INFLATION:
Causes, Consequences, Cures

INFLATION:
Causes, Consequences, Cures

*Discourses on the debate
between the monetary
and trade union interpretations*

LORD ROBBINS

SAMUEL BRITTAN

A. W. COATS

MILTON FRIEDMAN

PETER JAY

DAVID LAIDLER

With Addenda by

F. A. HAYEK

PETER JAY

and contributions to the Discussion by

MICHAEL ALISON

JOHN FLEMMING

RICHARD HENDERSON

RUSSELL LEWIS

A. J. MERRETT

EDGAR PALAMOUNTAIN

GORDON T. PEPPER

NICHOLAS RIDLEY

J. R. SARGENT

GEORGE SCHWARTZ

Published by

**The Institute of Economic Affairs
1974; Third Impression 1976**

First published in 1974 by

THE INSTITUTE OF ECONOMIC AFFAIRS

Second Impression 1975

Third Impression 1976

© The Institute of Economic Affairs 1974

SBN 255 36063-0

Printed in England by
Goron Pro-print Co. Ltd., Lancing, Sussex

Contents

	Page
PREFACE	vii
1. CAUSES, EFFECTS, DEVELOPMENTS	1
Lord Robbins	
Prospects	4
Depression with rising prices?	5
Now is not time to reflate	6
Oil prices: a theoretical analogy	7
A gloomy picture	8
2. INFLATION IN PERSPECTIVE—AN HISTORIAN'S VIEW	11
A. W. Coats	
Selection	13
Interpretation	14
Monetary explanations	16
Causes and effects	17
Diametrically opposed conclusions	18
The current inflation	19
Economic literacy	20
Historical record comforting	21
DISCUSSION	21
3. DO TRADE UNIONS MATTER?	25
Peter Jay	
The current debate	27
The monetary solution	28
Monetarists' ambivalence	30
Caveat concedes the case	31
All-important policy difference	33
US and UK: are the facts different?	34
DISCUSSION	35

4. THE CRISIS—WHEN AND WHY DID IT START?   51
David Laidler
  Post-war British inflation   53
  'Going-for-growth'   55
  Monetary contraction   55
  The frustration hypothesis   58
  More inflation to come   59
  Good and bad economics   60
  DISCUSSION   60

5. INFLATION, TAXATION, INDEXATION   71
Milton Friedman
  Taxation without representation   73
  The technicalities of indexing   74
  The Keynesian theory   76
  Voluntary indexation   77
  Escalator clauses   78
  The financial intermediaries   79
  Indexing and authoritarianism   81
  DISCUSSION   81

6. INFLATION AND GOVERNMENT   89
Samuel Brittan
  Imperfections of the political market   91
  'Mass unemployment' scare   92
  Funny alliance?   93
  Indexation and a genuine floating rate   94
  DISCUSSION   95

SUMMING UP   104
Lord Robbins

ADDENDA
1. Inflation, Full Employment and the Threat to Democracy   107
   Peter Jay

2. Inflation: The Path to Unemployment   115
   F. A. Hayek

Preface

The *IEA Readings* have been devised to refine the market in ideas by presenting the varied approaches to a subject in a single volume. It is hoped they will be of special value to teachers and students of economics as well as to laymen who want to know what economists are thinking and writing on the subject that concerns them.

Readings number 14 reproduces the substance of remarks made by six speakers at a Seminar on *Inflation: Causes, Consequences, Cures*, revised or amplified in some cases, together with questions from the audience, the replies, and the general discussion between the speakers and the audience.

Professor Lord Robbins, who chaired the Seminar, began with a reference to a similar Seminar[1] in 1972, during which economists and others had emphasised the consequences of expansion in the supply of money then taking place, but whose warning went unheeded. He was followed by Professor A. W. Coats, of the University of Nottingham, who presented a brief but intriguing review of inflation in several episodes in history, which made some of the audience wish he had spoken longer. He has amplified his spoken text a little here and there and added sources for the special benefit of students and teachers of economics and economic history.

The third speaker was Mr Peter Jay, the Economics Editor of *The Times*, who identified four main 'schools' of thought—Marxist, Keynesian, Hayekian and Friedmanite—and joined issue with the Friedmanites, arguing that trade unions, at least in Britain, can play a key role in the causation of inflation. Much of the subsequent discussion revolved around the degree of emphasis assigned to the supply of money and to the trade unions. Mr Jay's remarks echoed a diagnosis he had offered, in *The Times* of 1 July, 1974, of economic instability or disequilibrium between the four objectives of full employment, stable prices, free collective bargaining, and parliamentary democracy.

The fourth speaker, Professor David Laidler, of the University of Manchester, one of the leading monetarists in Britain, argued his case strongly, and with illustration from recent history. He was powerfully reinforced by the world leader of the monetarist school, Professor Milton Friedman.

---

[1] *Inflation: Economy and Society*, Readings No. 8, IEA, 1972.

The final speaker, Mr Samuel Brittan, reviewed the main arguments during the day, and drew some lessons for policy-making.

Not the least interesting—and, especially for students, valuable—aspect of this collection is that, apart from the formal presentation of opinion from the six main contributors, about a half of the material comprises stimulating exchanges between the speakers or between them and the audience, which included economists, economic journalists, and people in government, industry and finance.

The addresses and interchanges touched on the elementals of the economic theory of inflation as well as on the practicalities confronting government in mastering it. Students will find that the speakers combined analysis of the fundamental theories with informed discussion of the urgency of practical action. Not least was the discussion, towards the end of the day, of the nature of the 'cause' (or 'causes') of inflation, of the very meaning of a 'cause', the difference between proximate and ultimate causes, between the mechanism or instrument of money supply and the deep-lying institutional or structural elements, such as the trade unions, the continuing thirty-year-old attachment to 'full' or 'high' employment as the primary aim of policy, the commitment to high government expenditure on state welfare, etc., or any others which induce or compel governments to inflate by expanding the supply of money. The volume will thus be of interest to economists and to people in industry and government.

In addition to the material based on the proceedings in the Seminar, the collection includes two addenda. Addendum 1, an article from *The Times* of 1 July, 1974, by Mr Jay (by kind permission of the Editor and the author), is included because it amplifies the references in his contribution to the difficulties of reconciling the four desirable but arguably irreconcilable objectives. Addendum 2, a two-part article by Professor F. A. Hayek from the *Daily Telegraph* of 15 and 16 October, 1974, is included (by kind permission of the Editor and the author) to elucidate the reference by Mr Jay to Hayekian views of the role of money supply and the trade unions in the causation of inflation.

The Institute is grateful to the six main participants as well as to the questioners and others in the audience who joined in the discussions.

The volume offers its readers rich fare from some of the most distinguished economists and economic expositors of the Western world.

October 1974   EDITOR

1. Causes, Effects, Developments

LORD ROBBINS

THE AUTHOR

LORD ROBBINS: sometime Professor of Economics, London School of Economics and Political Science. Director of Economic Section of the offices of the War Cabinet, 1941 to 1945. Chancellor of Stirling University. Chairman of the *Financial Times*, 1961 to 1971.

Ladies and Gentlemen,
It is now some two years since we held a conference here in this building under the same auspices as our hosts today—The Institute of Economic Affairs, which has done so much to promote sane discussion and exchange of views on matters of important public business; and our subject was the same as today's, namely inflation.

In the last few days I have been looking up the record; and I must say we do not come out badly.

As regards the effects of inflation, we were in substantial agreement that they were bad. We agreed that they involved injustice in distribution *via* the impoverishment of those with fixed incomes. We agreed that they played havoc—very dangerous havoc—in company accounting and planning: we certainly anticipated the liquidity difficulties of the present day. We agreed that they impaired industrial relations in promoting a wild struggle to keep up with, and anticipate changes in, the purchasing power of the pay packet. And we agreed that they had disquieting effects on public morale and that these effects were likely to get worse.

As regards the causes of the inflation there was less agreement. There was a certain amount of shyness about something which was labelled 'monetarism', a concept which can have a tight or more elastic interpretation; and there was at least one distinguished speaker who denounced it with bell, book and candle. Some people were inclined to attribute our troubles to international causes, so that we could provide some sort of let-out for our much harassed politicians in that way. And of course there were many who emphasised the role played in the business of collective bargaining by associations of producers. But all, I think, even including the anti-monetarists, agreed that the increase of the credit base (although it might not be described as your strict monetarist would describe it, as *the* cause of the inflation, nothing else mattering) at a rate faster than the rate of increase of GNP was a condition of the continuation of inflation.

Alas, the course of history shows that intelligent discussion only influences the conduct of affairs after a very long period, if at all. As we all know, no attention was paid to our deliberations by those who rule over us. Instead, shortly after that, a prices and incomes policy (a policy about which, let me emphasise, in my judgement

3

intelligent people can take two views) was adopted. But despite the fact that a prices and incomes policy only has a ghost of a chance if it is not accompanied by some brake on the financial inflationary process, those who rule over us began deficit financing on a scale I believe unprecedented in the history of this country in peacetime. And they defended themselves—I am now quoting Mr Barber—on the ground that we need no longer trouble about the rate of exchange since it was floating.

Now I am betwixt and between in the matter of the exchange rate. I was at Bretton Woods and therefore I have a little emotional fixation on that system of adjustable rates rather than one which is floating all the time. And I have written quite a lot about it. I always think that when one writes about some subject, one ought not to flinch from the unbearably banal; and so I always used to say that, if the rate were floating, Ministers would say that it would take care of itself. I assure you it gives me no pleasure at all to see these predictions so abundantly borne out. So the result of all this has been a quickened rate of inflation, an adverse balance of payments which even before the operations of the oil cartel was unprecedentedly bad, an external position which has only been sustained so far by vast overseas borrowing against assets which are yet to be productive, interest rates at an all time 'high' because people have at last tumbled to the difference between money rates and real rates, liquidity crises galore, famous names from famous firms appearing week after week in the *Financial Times* and elsewhere as being in difficulties. And public morale at an ebb much lower, I think, than even the most pessimistic of us would have expected at that time.

Prospects

What is the present position and what are the prospects? One has to remember that inflation operates with a certain time-lag. I am not in a position myself to provide an intellectual explanation in detail of the *modus operandi* of the time-lag. But I think, empirically speaking, it is quite clear that it takes some time to get through. In the United Kingdom I am sure that we are still suffering and shall continue to suffer—even if very wise and rational policies are adopted here and now—from what has been done to us in the last two years. The powerful OECD has predicted that prices in this country are going to rise at the rate of 20 per cent per annum in the next year. They did not divulge their sources in this exact prediction, and I am not prepared to underwrite it. But I am prepared to guess that the direction of movement is going to be of a disturbing order of magnitude.

At the same time—and here one must give some credit, at any rate qualified, to the present authorities, even the Chancellor of the Exchequer—the rate of increase of M3, the credit base, has been substantially diminished. I think it extremely unwise to attach too much importance to the last month's statistics—one has to have more figures than that to be able to talk with confidence; and it may be that the very low figures which appeared the other day were just freakish. But I suspect privately that the rate of diminution of the rate of increase has been at least as severe as severe monetarists would recommend. And some monetarists may feel that perhaps the rate has been a little hard.

Depression with rising prices?

Anyway, I am pretty clear that if this continues—and I hope that the general policy of diminution of the rate of increase will go on gradually—this, together with the existing liquidity crisis and all that, is going to cause the strange phenomenon of something like a depression accompanied by rapidly rising prices. And if, as may be expected, the so-called Social Contract does not work as well as some of its protagonists suggest, the claims for increased incomes which are likely to come along this winter will certainly make this contrast even more marked.

What are our safeguards? So far as politics are concerned, apparently the only safeguard that is held out by those ruling over us at the moment is this famous Social Contract, under which apparently, in return for some vague undertakings as regards wage claims, something called social justice will be achieved. This means in fact soaking the rich, the self-employed and the managerial class. I have no doubt that, if Mr Healey gets his way, that side of the social contract will be carried out with relish. But I am not quite so sure about the other side. And that is not because I think that the trade union leaders are a wicked set of people determined to bring the country to its knees and to wreck an ancient civilisation. They are paid to see that their members do not get a smaller rate of increase than the other chap; and when the wage structure has been upset by inflation as it has been upset already, it is only human nature that they will, to some extent at any rate, go on responding to the expectations of their members.

Now is not time to reflate

So the outlook is not a very happy one. Now what should we do? Basically, faced with this prospect, there are many people whom I like and argue with, with hat in hand, who are already crying —reflate! I must respectfully disagree. But first of all, before I state what would seem to me to be the commonsense ground for this recalcitrance, let me be quite clear about the management of M3. I personally hope that the policy will be cautious. In any case we shall have more bankruptcies than are yet in evidence. And I would say that a drop from an average rate of increase of something in the order of magnitude of 25 per cent to $12\frac{1}{2}$ per cent would be trying the structure of the economy pretty hard. In my judgement a desirable policy would be more gradual than that. But having safeguarded myself—although one can never safeguard oneself against the sort of cry 'sadistic deflationist!' and so on and so forth—let me go on to address myself to the general policy of reflation.

The first analogy which seems to me to need to be rubbed in is that *inflation is still taking place*. And reflation on any large scale can only make that worse. Is it really sensible, with prices rising at the rate which has been predicted, to be talking at large about reflation? Even if—a belief which may be entertained by quite sensible people—we think that some time ahead, if things get very much worse, there may be something to be said for easing up just a little, the only intelligible construction I can put on the really frantic calls for reflation in some quarters is the assumption that, whatever government is in power it is going to impose straight away an iron control of prices and wages. And that it will continue to be able to impose it despite reflation, which I think flies in the face of nearly all the empirical evidence so far.

Furthermore, those of my friends who urge measures of reflation seem to me to forget our international position. At present we are living to some extent on credit. We are mortgaging assets which have not yet come into production and we are doing that on a very large scale. I am not saying that something of that sort is not expedient. But the moment the rest of the world thinks we are going to re-inflate on any large scale, there is quite a lot of money which could move out of London at a very disturbing rate indeed. And let me say—and here I shall find myself in the disturbing position of rubbing up the wrong way the feelings of all sorts of people who I would like to think well of me—I do not think that the floating rate will take care of all that. I am not a completely fixed exchange rate man; I am certainly *not* in favour of going back to fixed rates *à la* Bretton Woods at this moment. But to those who comfort themselves with the thought that because the rate is floating it does not matter how much the hot money rushes out and so on, that side of things is okay I do say that the probable effect of a substantial fall from the present rate of sterling would simply be a rise in the cost of living, demands for higher wage rates than would otherwise have taken place, and consequently further progress into a condition of hyper-inflation.

Oil prices: a theoretical analogy

But this leads me to a point of theory. Here I must apologise to all the highbrow economic experts here, far ahead of the contemporary march of time, for these rather obvious remarks—there is a point of theory which I would like to ventilate. Some of the advocates of reflation now say that we ought to reflate because of the deflationary effects on our economy of the rise in price of oil. But, if this is correct, what is the theory on the subject? Let us suppose for a moment that there were no outside world and that something else had become scarce. Let us suppose that there had been some seismic disturbance which had cut off a very substantial part of the domestic coal supplies. There would be a shortage of energy and a rise in its price, if the price system were allowed to work at all. And suppose at the same time an enlightened government, if one could make that hypothesis, were committed to a policy of keeping the value of money stable. By hypothesis, because they had to pay more for the energy, people would have less to spend on other things. I ask: would it be appropriate, in the interests of keeping the value of money stable, to pump more money into the system so that they did not have less to spend on other things? It is not obvious to me that that would be so.

Now the rise in the price of oil for us is rather like that. We need to demand relatively less of imports or of the things that we can push into exports so as to earn more, to make the balance of payments

7

better in that respect. I ask: will an internal reflation to compensate for the rise in the price of oil facilitate that process of elimination? I am not against indexing some things—I see that Professor Friedman, who will be here later on, has already pronounced in favour of indexing government bonds and the tax system, and I am in agreement with him. But the policy of indexing all round breaks down a little when the rise in the cost of living, or whatever index you use, is due to *real scarcity* rather than *excess money*.

Of course there is a world problem created by the operations of this wretched oil cartel; and we have to accommodate ourselves to it for a few years in the absence of an international Sherman Act, which is not likely to come along. And there is a real problem if the transfer which is taking place to the oil countries as a result of their operation, is not spent; for then of course there would be deflationary influences in the world at large and quite exceptional measures might have to be improvised. But in our specially vulnerable position, with a rate of inflation still exceeding that of our main competitors, and with the volume of hot money now in London, I do suggest that, quite apart from the intractability of the internal situation, it is asking for trouble to lead the way in reflating to meet the international troubles due to increased oil prices.

A gloomy picture

I have given you a gloomy picture and I do not know any easy solution. I do not think any easy solution is going to come from the floods of specious oratory which we are going to hear in the coming election on all sides, but we can all go on thinking and talking. And in present circumstances I think the only thing for those of us who are not tied up with politics, is to urge in season and out of season three points in the hope that sooner or later they will get heard.

First, inflation will not cease if expenditure continues to outrun production.

Second, however skilfully managed, however carefully the brakes are applied, an inflation of this rate is not likely to be capable of being stopped without there being some depression of trade.

Third, the degree of unemployment which will be caused by a skilfully managed cessation of inflation will vary with the magnitude of the claims put forward and conceded.

I would say that, with the rate of exchange where it is now in relation to that of our competitors, and if there is not great international catastrophe in the next two or three years, there is no reason why the inflation could not be brought under eventual control without very great hardship. But I am not betting much on such a favourable outcome.

2. Inflation in Perspective— An Historian's View

A. W. COATS

*Professor of Economic and Social History,
University of Nottingham*

THE AUTHOR

A. W. COATS was born in 1924 and educated at Southall Grammar School, Bishopshalt School and University College, Exeter (now University of Exeter), where he graduated BSc(Econ) in 1948 and MSc(Econ) in 1950. He took further graduate work at the University of Pittsburgh, 1950-1, and the Johns Hopkins University, 1951-53, where he obtained his PhD. Since then he has been in the Department of Economic and Social History at the University of Nottingham, apart from one year at the University of York and periods as visiting professor in the USA at Virginia, Stanford, Columbia, and Wisconsin Universities. In 1958-9 he had a Rockefeller Fellowship in the USA, and during 1972-3 was Fellow of the Netherlands Institute for Advanced Study in the Humanities and Social Sciences at Wassenaar.

Professor Coats has written numerous articles in a wide variety of learned journals and has edited six books on economic history and the history of economic thought. He is currently undertaking research on the role of the economist in government since 1945, mainly in Britain.

12

In Kingsley Amis's novel *Lucky Jim* there is a professor who, when the 'phone rings, picks up the receiver and says 'History speaking'. I have a rather uncomfortable feeling that today I'm expected to 'speak for history'. Especially when I see alongside the title, which I admit I agreed to, the word 'Final'.* So you must not be surprised if this leads me to adopt a somewhat didactic and even moralising tone.

The temptation to do so is very great. At the present time history is being repeatedly raided by journalists, politicians, economists, and others seeking examples of inflation, or occasionally even deflation, either for rhetorical purposes, or to buttress an argument based on economic theory, political or ideological prejudice, or maybe even sheer personal anxiety. And it is the professional historian's duty not only to keep off this particular kind of bandwagon, but also to expose the abuse of history wherever it occurs.

Now, at this point I think it is appropriate to refer you to a wise philosopher who said that when a person begins a statement with the words: 'History proves that . . .' this should be interpreted to mean: 'I propose to assert without evidence that . . .' Disagreements among historians are perhaps less widely publicised, and usually less spectacular, than disagreements among economists. But they can nevertheless be profound. This is not to assert that there are no lessons of history: indeed, such an assertion would itself be a generalisation from which a lesson might be drawn. The trouble is that the lessons of history are often obvious and trivial—for example, the view that history never repeats itself, or at least never repeats itself exactly. As the cynic observed, it is only the historians who repeat themselves! And, of course, such lessons of history as there are must be expressed in very cautious and undramatic terms.

Selection

The present-day preoccupation with inflation is, of course, hardly surprising. Nor is it abnormal. In fact one popular writer on the subject wrote a chapter entitled 'Four Thousand Years of Rising

---

*['Final' indicated the title agreed with the speaker in place of one or two earlier working titles.—ED.]

Prices'.[1] And if we accept Milton Friedman's view that inflation is 'a steady and sustained rise in prices', this suggests that inflation is an inevitable state of affairs. Certainly there is nothing new about it. There are, of course, novel features in the present situation, some of which I shall mention later, with appropriate cautions and reservations. But in studying past inflationary experiences it is essential we appreciate that the facts do not 'speak for themselves', as some naive inductivists imply. Facts must be selected, arranged, and interpreted by the historian, or the economist if it is an economist looking to the past. There are no controlled experiments in the past to which we can go for tests of our theories.[2] And in this context it is appropriate to recall Mark Twain's witty but brutal observation that 'In real life the right thing never happens at the right place at the right time: it is the business of the historian to remedy this mistake'.[3] So, given this warning you will, quite properly, treat with some reserve any examples that may be selected for your benefit, either by me, or any other of today's speakers.

Interpretation

Apart from selection, the question of interpretation is even more delicate. At the present time many economists and historians are busy rewriting the history of prices in monetarist terms. Of course this kind of explanation of past price trends is not itself a new phenomenon. Broadly speaking, when I was taught 19th-century British economic history as an undergraduate, it was still fashionable to explain 19th-century price movements in largely monetary terms,

---

[1] Paul Einzig, *Inflation*, London: Chatto & Windus, 1952, Ch 2. By contrast, a recent writer in the *Economist* of 13 July, 1974, pp. 62-3, claimed that in Britain since 1661 'periods of falling prices have been more common than periods of rising ones'. However, he warned that 'comparisons between price levels over long periods are statistically a bit unreliable, but they are fun'.

[2] The historian's theories—whether explicit or implicit—help him to ask relevant questions, perceive significant relationships between facts, and make appropriate inferences where—as is often the case—the facts are uncertain or incomplete. The naive inductivist's faith in particular facts usually reflects a distaste for theory. Moreover, it is often an excuse for sloppy thinking based on unsystematic, implicit theorising which conceals the writer's preconceptions and prejudices and protects him from damaging criticism.

[3] I owe this reference to Professor Alan Musgrave, of the University of Otago, New Zealand.

especially by reference to changes in the supply and demand for the precious metals.[4] Then, for two or three decades there was a swing towards a more Keynesian type of interpretation, playing down the role of money and credit and emphasising changes in the volume and productivity of investment.[5] Similarly, nearly half a century ago the so-called 'price revolution' in 16th-century Europe was largely explained in monetary terms by reference to the Spanish acquisition of silver from America and its subsequent diffusion across Europe.[6] More recently it has been shown that there are serious deficiencies in that account, since the timing, geographical location and extent of price movements are not compatible with the requirements of a broad quantity theory explanation.[7] Of course, it could not be said that changes in the volume and productivity of investment were of critical importance in the 16th century; consequently historians have not adopted a simple Keynesian explanation. Some, however, have turned to demographic factors, arguing that the most convincing explanation of the price rise is the pressure of population growth on scarce resources at a time when technological progress was limited. This was especially true of agriculture, and the evidence that food prices rose more rapidly than the price of manufactured goods is cited in support of this contention.[8]

These examples serve as a reminder that historians are liable to re-interpret the past in the light of the ideas prevailing in their own

---

[4] The *locus classicus* of this view was W. T. Layton and G. Crowther, *An Introduction to the Study of Prices,* London, 1938.

[5] For example, in W. W. Rostow's *British Economy of the Nineteenth Century*, Oxford University Press, 1949.

[6] This view was especially associated with Earl Hamilton's *American Treasure and The Price Revolution in Spain, 1501-1650*, Cambridge, Mass., 1934, and his earlier article 'American Treasure and the Rise of Capitalism (1500-1700)', *Economica*, IX, 1929, pp. 338-57.

[7] For one admirable recent survey of the various explanations, R. B. Outhwaite, *Inflation in Tudor and Stuart England*, London: Macmillan, 1969. (This pamphlet was commissioned by the Economic History Society.) The author's conclusion is that 'over the period as a whole "real" factors, and especially the growing imbalance between the growth of population and agricultural output, offer the more satisfactory general explanation of inflation both in England and in Europe generally.' (*Ibid.*, p. 48.)

[8] An anti-monetarist economist, Professor Geoffrey Maynard, has particularly emphasised the dissimilar rates of agricultural and industrial development in his historical study, *Economic Development and the Price Level*, London: Macmillan, 1962.

time. But if this conveys the impression that they are merely the slaves of some 'defunct economist'—as policy-makers are reputed to be—then I am doing them an injustice. Such an interpretation would, in a sense, flatter them, since it might suggest that they try, and are able, to keep up with current or recent trends in economic theory. In practice, in so far as shifts in historical interpretation are attributable to changing economic ideas they tend to occur only after a substantial time-lag.

Monetary explanations

Nevertheless, given the recent resurgence of monetarist ideas and the current world-wide preoccupation with inflation, it will hardly be surprising if monetary explanations of historical phenomena come back into vogue in the next decade or so. In this context, by far the most significant leading indicator is the monumental *Monetary History of the United States, 1867-1960*, by Milton Friedman and Anna Jacobson Schwartz, published in 1963.[9] This volume exemplifies what may be termed economist's history, rather than historian's history. Whatever its intrinsic merits, the senior author's reputation was sufficient, by itself, to ensure that it would receive thorough and respectful attention. In the event, although some distinguished reviewers raised serious philosophical, methodological and theoretical objections, the study has been generally hailed as a masterly accomplishment, which sets new standards of historical scholarship in the monetary field. Needless to say, the general conclusions are entirely compatible with the monetarist viewpoint, of which Professor Friedman is by far the most renowned and vigorous exponent. But the volume is relevant here because it provides an outstanding example of the enormous intellectual fascination and the formidable difficulties of historical research in this area.[10]

---

[9] Published for the National Bureau of Economic Research by Princeton University Press, Princeton, N.J.

[10] The following reviews by outstanding economists, each of whom offers an unusual combination of high praise and penetrating criticism, will repay careful study by those who lack the time to read the original 800-page work: James Tobin, in *The American Economic Review*, Vol. 55, 1965, pp. 469-485; H. G. Johnson, in *The Economic Journal*, Vol. 75, 1965, pp. 388-396; Charles Goodhart, in *Economica*, Vol. 31, 1964, pp. 314-318; and Robert Clower, in *The Journal of Economic History*, Vol. 24, 1964, pp. 364-380.

Causes and effects

Generally speaking, there has been more disagreement among historians and economists about the *causes* of inflation than about its *effects*. But even here, there is no unanimity of opinion, even in the case of hyper-inflation, which is often regarded as the worst of all possible inflationary worlds.[11] Perhaps the best-known example of this phenomenon occurred in post-World War I Germany, when the mark fell from around eight to the dollar in December 1918 to 4,200 milliards to the dollar in December 1923. During the same period, the note issue rose from about 35 millions to around 600 millions. According to the classic study of this episode by an Italian economist, Bresciani-Turroni, originally published in 1931 and translated into English in 1937, this was a period of extreme misery and unexampled social injustice, which benefited a small, but politically powerful group, and was largely responsible for the subsequent catastrophic economic and political developments, including the Great Depression of the early 1930s and the victory of the Nazi movement.[12] This is, of course, an abbreviated and over-simplified account; but the Bresciani-Turroni version was widely accepted in subsequent decades, and the English translation was reprinted in 1953, without revision or amendment.

Ten years later, however, two Scandinavian economists, Karsten Laursen and Torgen Pedersen, published a very different interpretation of the German post-war experience in which they attributed the disaster to the *restrictive* monetary policies imposed on Germany by other countries.[13] While not denying the seriousness of the hard-

---

[11] It is customary to regard an annual price rise of about 4 per cent per annum as moderate or 'creeping' inflation, whereas hyper-inflation involves a price rise of more than 50 per cent per *month:* cf. M. Bronfenbrenner, 'Inflation and Deflation', *International Encyclopedia of the Social Sciences*, New York: Macmillan & Free Press, 1968, Vol. 7, pp. 289-301. This authoritative essay has a useful bibliography, and may be instructively compared with the earlier essay on the same topic by James Harvey Rogers and Lester V. Chandler in the *Encyclopedia of the Social Sciences*, New York: Macmillan, 1932, Vol. VIII, pp. 28-33.

[12] Constantino Bresciani-Turroni, *The Economics of Inflation* (trans. M. E. Sayers), London: Allen & Unwin, 1937. It is worth noting that the English version contained an introduction by our Chairman, Lord Robbins.

[13] *The German Inflation 1918-1923*, Amsterdam: North Holland Publishing Co., 1964: '. . . the German inflation took place because the sacrifices called for by

Continued on page 18

ships caused by the hyper-inflation, they argued that the adoption of a deflationary policy would have brought grave political upheavals, possibly even a revolution; and it was the fear of revolution that led the Government to expand the money supply. The supposed damage to the productive mechanism from the resulting rise in prices was much less grave than Bresciani-Turroni and others had maintained, and even the redistributive effects were less serious than generally assumed because there was a high level of production and employment during the hyper-inflation.[14]

Diametrically opposed conclusions

My purpose in referring to this conflict in historical interpretation is not to take sides, but to illustrate the general contention that historians and economists undertaking careful studies of inflationary episodes can reach diametrically opposed conclusions, and to suggest that broad shifts in prevailing economic views help to account for these differences. Historians are disciplined by the evidence which, though usually limited and difficult to interpret, imposes definite constraints upon flights of historical imagination— constraints which are less evident in undergraduate essays and some newspaper columns! And it is precisely this kind of discipline which explains the delightful remark attributed to one of Jane Austen's characters: 'I often think it odd that history should be so dull, for a great deal of it must be invention'.

The professional historian is always on guard against those using the past to account for present discontents, if only because of the almost irresistible tendency to rely on mono-causal explanations of complex phenomena. In the case of inflation, concentration on the

---

[13]—*Continued from page 17*

policies based on the prevalent monetary theory were unbearable . . . the inflation was much to be preferred to the subsequent instability and to the other evils . . . which were due, not to the inflation, but to the measures applied to combat it. It was an erroneous monetary theory that induced the Anglo-Saxon powers, and with them the neutral countries of North-Western Europe, shortly after the end of World War I ruthlessly to balance their budgets, mercilessly to subdue economic expansion in order to prevent prices from rising and to return to the pre-war parity with dollars' (p. 10). The anti-monetarist tone of this passage is clear enough.

[14] For a summary of their conclusions, *ibid.*, pp. 123-7.

money supply, trade unions, or any other single factor is invariably a sign of over-simplification. In explaining sustained or severe inflations it is necessary to consider the entire political and social context, for one of the lessons of history is that governments can control rising prices if they so desire. But, as Laursen and Pedersen point out, the cost of doing so may seem politically and socially intolerable. The wisdom of hindsight and casual empiricism suggests that if an attempt is to be made to check inflation, the sooner the better is a wise prescription. But it is a prescription easier to give than to receive.

The current inflation

Viewing the current inflation in historical perspective, certain distinctive features stand out—though it must be emphasised that the following remarks are no substitute for a thorough analysis of the situation.

Lord Robbins has suggested that in Britain now we are witnessing an inflation unprecedented in peacetime; and it would certainly be difficult to demonstrate that this movement is merely a belated legacy of World War II. The global extent of the current price rise (that is, outside the communist countries) may be unique; but it is no surprise, for it reflects the growth of international economic interdependence during the past century or so. As a result, few national economies are insulated from major world economic trends, though it is clear from the experience of the inter-war years that depression can inspire determined efforts to devise schemes of national self-sufficiency and so-called 'beggar-my-neighbour' policies.

During the past three decades there has been a virtually continuous growth in government economic activity, involving a rising ratio of public expenditure to Gross National Product and an increasing assumption of state responsibility for economic management. Keynesian economics has, of course, directly contributed to these unprecedented developments, but it is absurdly flattering to the economists to regard them as the principal architects of the present crisis. Economists are the servants, not the masters of governments, and the change in public attitudes towards economic policy since the 1930s, though undoubtedly influenced by Keynes and his followers, reflects a deep-rooted and generally accepted conviction that depressions and large-scale unemployment are avoidable evils.

Given this belief—whether right or wrong—no democratic government can afford to permit substantial or lasting unemployment if it wishes to remain in office.

There has, in other words, been a fundamental shift in the public's economic expectations which reflects an underlying change in political and social values. In the post-war period the avoidance (or minimisation) of unemployment has tended to take precedence over other economic objectives, so that until quite recently expressions of concern about rising prices came mainly from those who feared that continued inflation would eventually produce the slump and unemployment which has so far been successfully avoided in leading industrial nations. Now at last we appear to be faced with a choice between evils—unemployment or runaway inflation; and the gloomier prophets among us fear that these may not be mutually exclusive alternatives.

Economic literacy

Another distinctive feature of the present situation, one that is potentially dangerous in a period of rapidly rising prices, is the extent of economic awareness among members of the general public. However much we may complain about the quality of economic journalism, or the level of economic literacy and political acumen of our politicians, 25 years of balance-of-payments crises, stop-go policies, wage freezes, prices and incomes controls, and the like, have made important sections of the community much more sensitive to economic affairs than ever before. While it is currently fashionable, and by no means unreasonable, to say that we are in the midst of the worst economic crisis since the war, and perhaps since the 1930s, there is little evidence of a collective willingness to make the individual or collective sacrifices which, it is constantly said, are so urgently needed. Nor is there any clear sign of a slackening of the rising economic expectations which 30 years of depression-free growth and expanding government activity have engendered. It is perhaps too soon to say that we may 'talk ourselves into' a collective neurosis, with a collapse of confidence, a flight from the currency, and a hyper-inflation. But the longer the present situation continues, the stronger the likelihood of such an outcome.

Historical record comforting

Fortunately for me, in circumstances like this I can always emphasise that I am an historian, not an economist. Consequently, prediction and prescription are no part of my business. Nevertheless, in times of crisis many people turn to the past, either for consolation, guidance, or merely as an escape from pressing anxieties. The historical record provides some comfort for those seeking it. By comparison with previous experience our present inflation is far from extreme. It is much closer to the 4 per cent per annum of creeping or moderate inflation than to the 50 per cent per month of hyper-inflation. Moreover, despite the grave limitations of our knowledge, we have learnt a good deal in the past 30 years or so about the techniques of economic management, and we have contemporary examples, like that of Chile—with an inflation rate exceeding 500 per cent per annum during the past two years—to serve as an awful warning of what we must avoid.

It may therefore be appropriate to finish by reiterating George Santayana's solemn dictum, that those who cannot remember the past are condemned to repeat it.

DISCUSSION

SAMUEL BRITTAN—. . . What does Professor Coats regard as the essence of 'starting again'?

PROFESSOR COATS—In my view it is the will of the public to accept the new currency as a valid means of exchange. And this means that the political and social tensions which have built up in the previous hyper-inflation episodes became intolerable and are generally recognised to be so, and also that the will of the government to restrict the money supply and the new currency has been fairly widely recognised. Otherwise I see no reason why there should not be a flight from the new currency, in a similar way as with the previous currency. It is not a profound answer but it seems to me there is a fundamentally non-economic explanation why such a process is successful.

RUSSELL LEWIS[1]—As I remember the classic work on the subject is by Earl Hamilton who said that the Spanish inflation was caused by the import of precious metals from the New World via Seville which had the import monopoly. Does that not still stand?

PROFESSOR COATS—I think it clearly does not stand. I think the evidence suggests that the timing of rising prices in other countries was not directly connected. For example, in this country it appears that prices were rising quite sharply even before any significant quantities of Spanish bullion came to this country, and that Hamilton generalised—after his famous book he wrote a number of articles about inflation in history. There is a tendency, when you make a successful effort like this and people receive it widely, simply to apply it to the whole of human history. A lot of research has been done to show that bullion was coming in through other ports, and that even in Spain itself the rise in prices was not as simple as Hamilton suggested. But particularly when you examine western and northern Europe you have to study the patterns of trade, communications with Spain, and so on—I can refer you to recent sources on this subject.

LORD ROBBINS—Do you not think that members of the audience would be well advised to read the *Discourse on the Commonwealth of England*? I have always regarded it as one of the most thrilling documents of the contemporary Elizabethan scene. It is a dialogue and the participants put forward all sorts of explanations of contemporary problems. At the time it was written by whoever wrote it—whether Smith or Hale—there was debasement and the repercussions of debasement, which is a kind of inflation. But by the time it was published the man who edited it added an explanation of prices on quantity theory lines. His conclusion was that somehow or other if increased supplies of precious metals had not come forward the position would have been rather different. Whether he had got this from Bodin or whether he had thought it out for himself is not known.

MICHAEL ALISON[2]—I wonder if I could go back to your introductory remarks, Lord Robbins, to focus on the interesting

---

[1] Economic journalist; author of Hobart Paperback No. 3, *Rome or Brussels . . . ?*, IEA, 1971.

[2] Under-Secretary for Health and Social Security, 1970-74.

picture you have presented of the closed economic community in these islands and the seismic event which suddenly produced a sharp contraction of the quantity of coal. Suppose the seismic event was not such as to produce a shortage of coal but a comparable event which gave coal-miners an extraordinary power to raise their wages; and not only the coal miners but other powerful unions. Would the same theory apply for a government wishing to maintain the stability of the currency? Should it nevertheless not in any way compensate by increasing the quantity of money over and above that quantity which was going to be diverted to those unions?

LORD ROBBINS—No, on the contrary, I should say that, if they did increase the quantity of money in response to this monopolistic pressure, they would be well on the way to inflation. I should have thought that the appropriate method for dealing with monopolistic exactions in a closed community is to apply the monopolies and restrictive practices legislation.

QUESTIONER*—If I could go back to the question of the current inflation, does it not depend to some extent on a loss of confidence? Given the degree of awareness now of current economic affairs, is there not something that could be done to reverse the distrust of money which is certainly one of the factors driving up prices?

LORD ROBBINS—I agree that confidence is essential. But that will not return until people believe that the government will do the right things regarding the currency. Given that belief, there is at once created a wider elbow-room for policy. Schacht pulled it off in the German currency reform after the First World War by calling his new money the Rentenmark which assumed the kind of backing which wasn't there and in any case would have been inappropriate. But everyone was sick of the old currency and they were in a frame of mind to trust anything to get away from that.

PROFESSOR COATS—I would say that, if you think economic literacy makes you more distrustful of governments in general, your point holds. But, if increased economic understanding makes you realise that fundamentally confidence in money is essential, it would seem to me you could argue the other way: that people realise increasingly that you must have a stable monetary unit. Perhaps one

---

*[Owing to the imperfections of the tape recording of the Seminar, some of the questioners could not be identified.—ED.]

could argue, even more fancifully that, with widespread economic literacy, people could devise alternative means of payment than a government-backed unit of currency.

LORD ROBBINS—Supposing we had, in this country, a new pound, a not altogether fanciful possibility three or four years hence. If they were able to give convincing political guarantees that they were not going to increase the credit base at more than a percentage per annum sanctioned by professional experts, I guess there might be some slight revival of confidence.

3. Do Trade Unions Matter?

PETER JAY

Economics Editor, 'The Times'

THE AUTHOR

PETER JAY has been Economics Editor of *The Times* since 1967. He was born in 1937 and educated at Winchester College and Christ Church College, Oxford, where he gained an M.A. with First Class Honours in PPE in 1960; in that year he was President of the Union. From 1961 to 1967 he was in the Civil Service at the Treasury. He has been Associate Editor of *The Times Business News* since 1969, and presenter of the Sunday morning ITV programme, *Weekend World,* since 1972. He has written a book, *The Budget,* published in 1972.

He is a son of the Rt Hon Douglas Jay, MP, and is married to a daughter of the Rt Hon James Callaghan, MP, and has three children.

Let me put your minds immediately at rest by assuring you that I shall not answer the question.

But I genuinely want to know the answer to this question. I think everybody here will be familiar with the debate which is suggested by this self-explanatory question, 'Do trade unions matter?'

I think it is worth noting that it is not a debate, as sometimes suggested, between Keynesians and monetarists. There are in fact two groups of people who think that trade unions do not matter— by 'matter' I mean 'matter to the process of inflation'. One group is the very distinguished group led by Professor Friedman himself; and the other group comprises the Marxists and the almost Marxists. They too strongly maintain, like the Friedmanites, that trade unions are not and cannot be a continuing, pervasive cause of inflation.

It is interesting really to arrange opinions on this question across a spectrum which has four nodal points. These I shall, no doubt inaccurately, label as Marxist, Keynesian, Hayekian*—I suspect that that description is indifferently accurate—and finally, though I use the term with extreme diffidence in this situation, Friedmanite.

The current debate

We are all here familiar with the way in which this debate has cropped up in our own arguments about economic policy, most vigorously of late. People may have followed the exchanges between Sir Keith Joseph, Lord Kahn, Mr Reginald Maudling and others which have taken place in the columns of one of our daily newspapers. The position was strongly taken there by Lord Kahn not only that trade unions do matter, but also that collective bargaining in the form in which we have had it is a, perhaps the, most pervasive, persistent cause of post-war inflation. Moreover, he maintained that this argument was not a semantic one, but of great importance.

I myself think that it probably is one of great importance, although I think that the way in which it has been conducted is in danger on occasions of concentrating on what is a semantic point. I think it is important for the following reasons. And I am here concentrating on that frontier in the debate which lies between what I have loosely

*[The Hayekian view as stated most recently by Professor F. A. Hayek in the *Daily Telegraph* is reproduced here as Addendum 2, p. 115.—ED.]

called the Hayekians and the Friedmanites. That particular frontier may be of special interest to us here. It is certainly the one which is of greatest interest to me.

It is essentially an argument between two groups of people both of whom regard themselves as in some sense monetarists, both of whom think that the money supply is the most important single control variable available to them, or at least to the authorities, in affecting the short-term behaviour of the real variables in the economy and the long-term behaviour of the monetary variables in the economy.

Now the reason why it is important, it seems to me, is this. If you think that trade unions have the capacity by collective bargaining to raise the general level of pay and that by so doing they confront governments with a choice between *either* continuing with what in normal circumstances one would regard as a non-inflationary monetary policy, in which case the trade unions will have priced themselves out of the labour market and unemployment will result, *or*—if the government has a commitment as most governments, certainly our governments, have had ever since the war—not to allow unemployment to rise even in the short term, intervening in the process with what I think we would call inflationary increases in the money supply thereby igniting the process by which inflation starts, then there is a sense in which trade unions can cause inflation and no sense in which their behaviour is irrelevant to the politics and economics of counter-inflationary policy in a democracy.

Everybody here will be familiar with that argument and with the argument that such a combination of monopoly bargaining and political commitment to full employment is bound to lead to accelerating inflation, as the pay bargains in the next round allow for the increase in prices in the last round and maybe even extrapolate them into the future, building them into the next set of demands and so on *ad infinitum*.

The monetary solution

Now if that is correct, what would be the consequences of applying a non-inflationary monetary policy, as recommended by Professor Friedman? The sophisticated version of it, as I understand it, would be that one would move gradually back from the excessive rates of increase in money supply towards non-inflationary increases in the money supply. The consequences that, as I understand it, one would then expect to occur would be that over the short term there would be a recession in the real variables in the economy. Output would begin to fall in relation to capacity. A GNP gap would develop; and it would grow. This process would continue, on the assumptions which I have described, until there was a balance in the economy between, on the one hand, the inflationary—if you like, monopolistic—bargaining powers of organised labour and, on the other hand, the weakness in the demand for labour, in the sense that pay increases in excess of the growth in productivity ceased to occur.

Now if the Hayekian model is correct, this equilibrium will be stable. From that point on what one would expect would be that prices would be stable, productivity as determined by non-monetary factors would continue to advance along its normal course and output would grow in line with it. The monopolistic bargaining power of organised labour would remain what it was, balanced by the weak demand for labour, and the economy would be stable at a permanent level of unemployment well above that which we have customarily come to call full employment in the post-war period. I do not think there is any empirical work, or indeed speculation, which enables us with much confidence to say what that level would be. One man's opinion is probably as good as another's. It would, I believe, certainly be in the low millions. Some think it would be in the high millions.

Now, if that view about the capacity of organised labour through collective bargaining to push up the general rate of growth of pay faster than the rate of growth of productivity, when unemployment is below the equilibrium point which I have just described, is incorrect, then one would expect, following Professor Friedman's writings, that a temporary recession having developed, what Sir Keith Joseph calls the built-in stabilisers would begin to assert themselves. Inflation having been checked, the economy would then begin to move back towards—here I want to be very careful because I do not think that Professor Friedman has ever said 'full employment'— the 'natural' level of unemployment, which I suspect is widely and hopefully assumed to be not too far from full employment, though the evidence for this optimism is not entirely clear. Professor Friedman has been very rigorous about this. He says it depends on a number of factors which are nothing whatever to do with monetary policy and that, if there is a high degree of efficiency and competition in the labour market, the level may not be so very far above what we customarily regard as full employment.

Monetarists' ambivalence

So it is a real, not a semantic debate—about whether unemployment would or would not tend to fall in the circumstances described. Now I have no intention of seeking to resolve it. But what I do wish to draw attention to is the fact that some British monetarists, who seek to follow Professor Friedman, have been ambivalent on this question whether or not trade unions matter. They have not always taken the pure, self-consistent position which Professor Friedman takes. They have shilly-shallied, I think, between the two sides of the debate. I think it is right that we should draw attention to this ambivalence. In the course of the shilly-shallying, or in the course of making what they have themselves described as one or two important caveats, they have I think conceded the whole argument to the other side of the case.

I would draw attention here in particular to the writings, and I cite him only because he is a particularly distinguished exponent of this point of view, of Professor Alan Walters, both in his Aims of Industry pamphlet and in letters he has written to the press and, particularly on this occasion, in the pamphlet *Dear Prime Minister*[1] to which he contributed, though he was not the sole author. Since Professor Laidler here is also one of the distinguished authors of this work, I have no doubt that he will be able to give a full exegesis of the difficulty which appears to arise. In the opening of this pamphlet it is stated that, 'It has also been our purpose [that is, the purpose of this group of people addressing themselves to the Prime Minister who I think can loosely be called monetarists of one kind or another] to refute the notion of wage inflation and the need for a prices and incomes policy'.[2] That appears to me to be a fairly straightforward statement that trade unions do not matter in the sense in which we are discussing them here this morning.

On the other hand, if you turn to a later passage in this work, on page 6 of the copy I have, it is stated that there is, however, an 'important caveat'; and the caveat is as follows:

---

[1] Economic Radicals, London, 1974.
[2] *Ibid.*, p. 1.

'If the increase of union wages induces the authorities to expand the money supply either to finance public expenditure designed to reduce any concomitant unemployment or to finance the deficits of nationalised industries then such action will indeed be inflationary. It is simply not possible for the trade unions to be so powerful as to cause prices to rise generally unless there is concomitant increase in the money supply. No-one has ever produced any evidence to the contrary'.

Caveat concedes the case

Now it seems to me that this caveat concedes the whole of the case to those whom I loosely described as Hayekians. The mechanism which those monetarists who say that trade unions do matter have believed to operate is precisely that mentioned in the caveat, namely that in the post-war era in Britain, mildly during the first 20 or so years, but much more powerfully in the period from the autumn of 1969 onwards, organised labour has had just this capacity, by increasing general pay levels faster than productivity increases, to induce the authorities to expand the money supply. It induces the authorities to expand the money supply for exactly the reason given here, namely that they wish to reduce any concomitant unemployment. And the reason why they wish to reduce any concomitant unemployment is that they have been committed ever since 1944 in this country, ever since the 1946 Employment Act in the United States, not to allow concomitant unemployment to occur.

Therefore it seems to me that the more useful formulation of the point is to say that, in conditions where you have a commitment against unemployment even in the short term, in conditions where you have free collective bargaining with the capacity—and a capacity which is indeed being used—to cause the general pay level—and I emphasise again the *general* pay level—to rise faster than productivity, then governments have a straight choice: either to break their commitment to full employment or to issue inflationary finance. And, given that they do not wish to break the commitment, they then issue the inflationary finance and the inflation results.

Now, it seems to me a semantic question whether or not one feels it is correct in this context to say that it is the increase in the money supply which causes the inflation and that all the trade unions are doing is merely forcing the government or putting great pressure on the government to take such action, or to say, as would seem to me more straightforward, that it is indeed the actions of trade unions in this general context, with the other assumptions, which are causing the inflation. It is not necessarily an unimportant question. It is a question about which Professor H. L. A. Hart, the former Professor of Jurisprudence at Oxford, has, not in this but in another context, written at some length and with great learning, namely the question precisely how we use the concept of causation when talking in this kind of way. That, to put your minds at rest, is not a subject into which I intend to go any further, but I wish at least to suggest to you that the problem is of that kind.

And I think it would be very helpful to hear not only from Professor Friedman but also from Professor Walters and from Professor Laidler whether or not they accept that this is so. For, if it is so, if they accept the basic point however it is expressed, then it seems to me that the statement right at the beginning of *Dear Prime Minister* that they wish 'to refute . . . the need for a prices and incomes policy' becomes much more doubtful. If we accept that it is the paramount objective, or at least a major objective, that inflation should be checked, if we accept that it can be checked only by a package of policies which at least includes doing the right thing by the money supply, as Professor Friedman would recommend, and if we further accept that the consequences of doing so are that unemployment may rise, and if we further acknowledge the political facts of life in a democratic society—and not only a democratic society but also a society which is increasingly prone to express its dissatisfactions (not only dissatisfactions of the majority but also dissatisfactions of quite small minorities) in an extremely vigorous and sometimes rather daunting way—then I think one must recognise that, if it could be made possible to do the right thing by the money supply without those consequences, it would be a net gain, not only to the welfare of society, but also to the chances of seeing the anti-inflation policy through.

Now if the assumption, the basic assumption for Hayekians at least, about the UK economy is correct, namely that trade unions do indeed have this power, then it would presumably follow that, if they could be induced to refrain from exercising this power, or if, more radically, this power could be taken away from them (I put that in in order to placate my Nuffield College colleague—Mr Brittan), if one of those two things could be done, then the unemployment consequences would not result—or not in such acute form—and the policy would have a better chance of success. If that were true, then it would seem to me one would not be in the position of being able 'to refute . . . the need for a prices and incomes policy'. On the contrary, one would have demonstrated the need for a prices and incomes policy.

All-important policy difference

There is still, in the policy I am by implication suggesting, an all-important difference from the customary post-war policy as practised by all hues of politician: that, although I do not believe there need be any great difference of opinion between us as to what the *mechanisms* are, there is a very important difference between which *commitment* you make. If you commit yourself without qualification to maintain full employment and you seek to mitigate the operation of the collective bargaining mechanism by an incomes policy, it follows that, insofar as this policy is not successful, the residual is inflation, the strain is taken by inflation. If you commit yourself, by contrast, to an anti-inflation policy as the over-riding priority, then unemployment rather than inflation becomes the residual and takes the strain of incomes policy failure. The anti-inflation commitment does not have to be expressed in the monetary canon for this consequence to follow. It can be expressed in terms of a commitment to keep the rate of change of the money supply within a certain range. But, for the benefit of people who still find that language repugnant to their upbringing or understanding, it can equally well be expressed as a fiscal policy commitment, namely that through the budget one would seek to ensure that the rate of change of GNP at current prices (and I emphasise *current* prices) would be in line with the rate of change in productivity, or, if one was prepared to tolerate a minimal degree of permanent inflation, a little above. If you were starting from a position of high inflation, as we are, then one can also express the spirit of Professor Friedman's recommendation for gradualism in fiscal terms, namely that one should plan for a gradual decrease, year by year, in the rate of increase in GNP at *current* prices until such time as it was down to a non-inflationary level, i.e. in line with the rate of growth of productivity.

US and UK: are the facts different?

So, it seems to me that there are important and substantial questions of both theory and policy here, and that it hinges on whether trade unions matter. This argument between the Hayekians and Professor Friedman may depend upon empirical differences between the British and American economies. It may just be that the facts are different. I have heard Professor Friedman argue very persuasively that it is a question of theory, not facts, and that whatever the facts were, the conclusion could not be different. I still think that it is very difficult for people in Britain in the light of post-war experience and particularly in the light of what happened here in 1969 and 1970 to accept that this collective bargaining power does not exist, at least to the extent necessary to induce governments to take the kind of action which is allowed for in Professor Walters's caveat and which then leads on to inflation. So there is that important argument at that level.

But I suggest that there is no important argument between the positions taken by the British monetarists, at least as in their caveat in *Dear Prime Minister*, and by the Hayekians—or indeed the position taken by any Keynesian who wished to make the initial statement that higher priority should be given to checking inflation than to avoiding unemployment even in the short term. If there is an unperceived unanimity between these three groups, it is very important. For they embrace a really significant proportion of the whole range of debate about economic policy in Britain.

It certainly does not encompass every point of view. It does not encompass Mr Michael McGahey of the National Union of Mineworkers. It does not encompass Professor Friedman. But nonetheless it does encompass a very important group. Anyone who accepts, as the *Dear Prime Minister* caveat does accept, that trade unions in principle do have this power to force governments to choose between long-term inflation and short-term unemployment, and who also gives first priority to stopping inflation, whether he calls himself fiscalist or monetarist, belongs to that important group. They have no real *casus belli* amongst them and should concentrate on settling the question of either theory or fact which remains between them and Professor Friedman, or indeed the Marxists on the other side, whether or not that power of trade unions does indeed exist.

DISCUSSION

DAVID LAIDLER—I am anticipating a little what I have to say this afternoon; I do not want to get into what could end up as a semantic argument about what we really meant in a particular sentence, but let me say what I think about the role of trade unions in generating inflation.

I do not believe that in this country the trade union movement has any power whatsoever to raise the level of money wages in the absence of expansionary monetary policy. I will argue that proposition from the point of view of economic theory and of evidence. About half of the labour force of this country are members of trade unions, and the other half are not in trade unions; and of that 50 per cent a substantial number are in trade unions with no real monopoly power at all. What will happen if a trade union, in circumstances like that, uses its monopoly power to raise the level of money wages faster than the level of output? It will not cause general unemployment or a general rise in the price level. It will cause a diminution of employment in its own sector. Those who are not employed in it will swell the supply of labour to other sectors. The level of money wages in other sectors therefore will be lower, the structure of relative wages will be different, the structure of relative prices will be different. The general price level and the general wage level will not be different except to the extent that their index numbers are calculated in a particular way. That is the economic theory. Monopolistic trade unions have their effect on *relative* wages, and it is about time we stopped confusing relative real wages with the level of money wages. Second, empirical evidence. The most authoritative study that suggested trade unions could exercise an influence on the rate of inflation in this country independent of the level of aggregate demand was that of Professor Hines who published it in *The Review of Economic Studies* in 1963. His was a first-rate piece of work for its time.

If you take Hines's relationships and re-estimate them, updating them to 1969, not making any qualifications or any criticisms, taking his work at its face value, and ask what was the contribution of trade unions' so-called 'pushfulness' to price inflation in this country in the years 1968 and 1969—the answer is in 1968 it was nil and in 1969 1 per cent. And you will recognise that these are point estimates with standard errors around them. Lord Kahn has written an article in *The Times* asserting that trade unions have the power to fix money wages and that they are the key source of the current inflation. He may be right. He may have evidence that none of his professional colleagues in other institutions have seen. But if he has, I wish he would publish it in a learned journal where it can be properly refereed and then properly subjected to professional debate, before making assertions like that in *The Times*. We have published our evidence. He has not published his.

JAY—How about the caveat?

LAIDLER—I repeat the caveat. As I read it, it says that if trade unions are pushing up money wages at the same time as the government are permitting the money supply to increase, you get a rising money wage level. There is no evidence in this country that if you do not have an accommodating monetary policy, the trade unions have any power to raise money wages. Therefore it will follow that they have no power to increase the overall level of unemployment. I said I do not want to get into semantic debates about what we said might be read to mean.

LORD ROBBINS—Now clearly there's quite a lot to say about Professor Laidler's observations, but may we have some questions from the body of the hall?

EDGAR PALAMOUNTAIN[1]—At this moment we have, or at least a lot of laymen would think we have, a situation in which wage rates are going ahead very fast. At the same time the money supply is being far more rigorously controlled than it has been for many months, if not years. What are the implications?

JAY—I think the facts are that, at least until the last month or two when the figures began to move up again, the money supply—and it depends which measure you take and how you massage the figures, or which compromise you prefer, and so on—has during the last 12 months been rising at an annual rate of something like 10 per cent. Would that be wildly different from anybody else's estimate? I would not have thought so. Average earnings have been rising at an annual rate fairly closely in line with the rate of increase of prices, if anything rather faster. Therefore there is going to be a divergence between the two (money supply and earnings) over that period. If monetary theory is correct, with the usual lag, the behaviour of

---

[1] Deputy Chairman and Managing Director of the M & G Group.

money-GNP is related to the behaviour of money supply. If earnings within that total rise faster than the total then a shift from profit to pay must be taking place, or at least from some other category of incomes which looks like being profits in this case.

I do not think, though much greater authorities than I will correct me if I am wrong, that there is anything in monetary theory or in any particular theory of inflation which says that at a particular point in the cycle this cannot happen. On the face of it this is exactly what is happening. If you mean to ask what are the implications, not for theory but for policy, I would think they are fairly obvious. Companies, for this and other reasons, have a very acute liquidity problem at this moment. This reacts back on what is a genuinely important point in the theory of monetary policy—if I may put it that way—namely that another thing which is contributing to the extreme liquidity difficulties of companies, as the Bank of England *Bulletin* and Sir Keith Joseph and now this anonymous senior official spokesman of the National Westminster Bank have diagnosed it, is that the Bank of England, or let us say 'the authorities' in order not to be too pointed about it, have failed over the last months fully to take on board an important facet of Professor Friedman's writings. This is that if, from a position of very rapid monetary inflation, you move very suddenly to a position of non-inflationary increase in the money supply, or even of much less inflationary increase, you are likely to cause a rather serious financial convulsion which has various well-known symptoms such as sharp falls in asset values and bankruptcies in certain kinds of institutions which are dependent on the valuation of those assets, and so on.

It is therefore not at all surprising, I think, to a monetarist that, after such handling of the money supply by the authorities, there is indeed a financial convulsion of precisely the kind they would have predicted. I think their recommendation would be, as is suggested in the daily newspaper to which I have referred, that one should reduce the excess rate of increase in money supply more slowly. If you want to know how fast you should be increasing the money supply now, you should go back to where it was in mid-1973, deduct one or two percentage points a year, or something like that, and work out where you would be now—and move down from that point.

JOHN FLEMMING[2]—If autonomous demands by trade unions (of the kind mentioned by Professor Laidler) were to be highly correlated

---

[2] Fellow of Nuffield College, Oxford.

across the large number of trade unions that make up 50 per cent of the labour force who are members of trade unions, there might be a temporary increase in the level of unemployment. The government might be induced either to meet that in full by increasing the money supply, or to try and ease the cost of that transitional unemployment by raising the money supply.

Now there is some evidence, I believe, that recent wage demands have not been autonomous in this way. Many of the leading troubles on the labour front have been caused by the lagging behind of the wages of many organised workers. It is quite possible that the process which is started by an unwise monetary or fiscal policy on the part of the authorities should cause the wages of some people in the non-unionised sector to rise. This in turn leads to the exercise of existing powers on the part of those who are unionised, and in particular it leads to the spread of unionisation among those parts of the non-unionised sector not leading this process. You thus get added to the initial monetary disturbance the effect of increasing union pressure and the possibility therefore of the temporary unemployment associated with the adjustment of real wages, and so forth. So from this analysis, which may or may not be refuted by David Laidler's experiment with Professor Hines's equations, there would be a role for trade unions in the process of accelerating inflation or particularly an increase in the tendency to inflation and unemployment.

GORDON PEPPER[3]—The full monetarists' approach contains various elements which are designed to reduce the necessary rise in unemployment whilst inflation is being curtailed. A fall in the rate of growth of the money supply will be followed by a reduction in the rate of growth of money national income. Some of the reduction will be a fall in real economic activity, and a rise in unemployment, and part will be a reduction of inflation (the result of the direct monetary forces). It may be possible to bias the outcome in favour of a bigger reduction in inflation and away from a rise in unemployment with a prices and incomes policy that is definitely a temporary policy introduced at the same time as a serious attempt is made to control the money supply. For the same purpose Milton Friedman advocates

---

[3] A partner of W. Greenwell & Co., the stockbrokers, and principal author of Greenwell's *Monetary Bulletin*. Mr Pepper is a Fellow of the Institute of Actuaries.

a policy of index-linking wages. This is an extreme form of a prices and incomes policy. But many of us in this country are wary of index-linking wages because we need a fall in real wages to improve our balance of payments. A prices and incomes policy, although second best, may be the best practical measure of achieving the objective.

In a television interview last night Milton Friedman passed a motion in favour of index-linking government bonds. May I please ask Dr Friedman to differenciate very carefully between his advocacy of index-linking government bonds when the authorities *do* control the money supply and what happens if wages and the government bonds are index-linked but the government does not control the money supply. Whilst I would agree that index-linking government bonds is a very powerful weapon helping the Bank of England to control the money supply, if we have a continuation in the rise of the proportion of GDP absorbed by public expenditure, i.e. if the trend of the last few years continues during the next few years, I would not trust UK governments to control the money supply even if they sell index-linked government bonds. And that could be a disaster.*

RICHARD HENDERSON[4]—I am puzzled about the supposed benefits of statutory price and income controls. There seems to be an assumption which is widespread in many circles, and apparently in parts of this hall today, that there is some connection between a prices and incomes policy, on the one hand, and either the power of trade unions, or the ability of trade unions to exercise that power, on the other. I would have thought that there were serious empirical and theoretical objections to both these hypotheses. The empirical evidence, which in this country now goes back over a period of some ten years, I would have thought fairly clear. In terms of a theoretical argument one could imagine that, for example, the existence of a prices and incomes policy would dramatise the partly real and partly imaginary conflict between government on the one hand and unions on the other. It would therefore appear in the eyes of unionised or indeed non-unionised labour to increase the importance of belonging to a trade union and would therefore tend—if it had any effect at all —to increase the power of trade unions, given that trade unions have

---

* Mr Pepper's point was amplified and discussed by Professor Friedman later in the day (below, pp. 83–88).

[4] Economist working in research; a graduate of St Andrews.

power. I must say I fail to see any rational argument which persuades me that the mere passing of legislation in some way deprives the unions of the opportunity of exercising power. If they have the power and the inclination, that surely is the end of it. The idea, therefore, that controls can be used to moderate either unemployment or inflation by their effects on unions is something which I find difficult to understand. It is something of a paradox which I would be glad to have explained.

QUESTIONER—I gather that when one goes from expanding the money supply too fast down to a proper level, one is bound to get some unemployment, and much of the argument is how high that is going to be, and how reasonable the trade unions are. I suppose you might compare this to the 'drying-out' period of an alcoholic or the withdrawal symptoms of a drug addict. In this context it is often said we economists are flogging this view hard week after week, together with numerous other economic policies we ought to be ashamed of, that it will not work because you will get sit-ins and mass demonstrations, and so on. And there are rumours that Mr Heath is very frightened of this.

SAMUEL BRITTAN—Yes.

QUESTIONER—Thank you. Now, I would have thought that the essence of a strike is that you are depriving the community of something that people want. The essence of a sit-in is that you are depriving the community of something they do not want. Therefore, which is the more powerful? Nevertheless I wonder whether any of the panel —Mr Brittan or one of the other speakers—could tell us briefly, first, to what extent this fear does in practice affect politicians of both parties, and second, to what extent they think it ought to be entered into politicians' calculations?

LORD ROBBINS—It seems to me that, perhaps, without sufficiently sorting things out in order, we are discussing three separate questions which arise from the contributions of Peter Jay and David Laidler. The first question is: do we agree that, whether trade unions matter or not, control of the credit base is an indispensable condition of coping with inflation? I guess that public opinion or informed opinion is more unanimous than it was, let us say, two years ago. But it is an important question to keep clear in our minds.

Suppose we agree to that, there arises the second question: whether you can say that inflation is always caused by failure to observe prescription No. 1. David Laidler has argued, and I expect that Milton Friedman will argue, that, on his model, trade union power, if it were exerted, would be rather futile. Hayek was not the first economist to say that wages above the equilibrium point caused unemployment. But the so-called Hayekian position certainly calls David Laidler's position in question. I think I could construct a model which might enable some sort of concord . . . I suspect in the end that semantics do enter a good deal into the controversy.

First, assume there are no trade unions and there is sufficient control of the credit base. We may all agree that that would be okay: there would be no inflation. Then suppose trade unions arise but there is sufficient control of the credit base. What the unions try to do is likely, after a brief interval perhaps, to be pretty futile. But now introduce a new element in the model. The government is inspired by good will but is a little woolly, and there is no really effective mobility of labour between all areas in which the initial display of intransigence on the part of the trade unions might arise. They perceive that, for the time being, unemployment is created and they remember the pledges made in the coalition White Paper to maintain full employment, whatever that means, at whatever cost. So they tell the banks of England to go easy if industrialists then come along to them and say: 'We can't pay these wages'. Now whether this happened in the 1950s or 1960s on a very large scale is anybody's guess— there have been the most beautiful studies of economic management since the war, not only Professor Hines' but a wonderful study by Christopher Dow who is sitting in the audience. But I ask: is my model of this slightly woolly-minded government conceivable? And in that event what is '*the* cause', the woolly-mindedness of the government or the monopolistic power of the trade unions which led to the woolly-mindedness of the government to take this action of loosening up the money supply?

And the third question is whether a concession even of that sort to the so-called Hayekian point of view—this is what Peter Jay raised—would be an overwhelming argument for a prices and incomes policy. This raises the question of under what circumstances the prices and incomes policy can operate for long, and of course the further question whether, if it could be made to operate for long, it would be desirable. But I think we ought to keep these different things in mind. And perhaps when they come to make observations, David Laidler and Professor Friedman would address themselves to my little model.

MICHAEL ALISON—Would Professor Laidler kindly elaborate the picture of increased union pressure in one sector resulting in increased wages, leading to a shift of labour to other sectors where it would expand the supply and thus tend to reduce the wage level there, in other words the theory of relative wage movements? What are we to expect from very large settlements in the coal-mining industry and for nurses in terms of recruitment? He also seems to suggest that we should have fewer coal-miners and nurses. But this does not seem to be the purpose of the operation. Could you elaborate that.

DAVID LAIDLER—Yes, it is very simple. There are two kinds of wage increases. The first arises because the trade union has got some extra monopoly power and is further restricting the supply of labour into its sector to drive up wages—that's how unions can exercise their monopoly power. The second kind of wage increase, such as the miners and the nurses, is purely a matter of the workers in those particular sectors keeping up with inflation. The alleged generous offer made to the miners' union would still have left coal-miners with a predictable fall in their real income over the subsequent 12 months.

Lord Robbins talked about the woolly-minded government and the trade unions. Of course it is true that changes in the structure of trade union power can change the level of frictional unemployment. It is also true that if you increase council house subsidies you will reduce labour mobility and thereby perhaps increase the level of frictional unemployment. If you give security of tenure to furnished tenants, as we have just done, you will do the same. If the demographic structure of the labour force changes, the level of frictional unemployment will change. I have not heard anybody argue that these are factors leading to inflation.

The right approach is to say that governments have no business setting targets for a level of unemployment when they do not know whether those targets are attainable. Moreover, it is a real target. If you want a particular level of unemployment you had better tackle it with real policies like reducing the monopoly power of trade unions, affecting labour mobility by changes in the structure of housing subsidies, and so on. If you go after a real target with a monetary weapon, it is not surprising that you are going to fail to get it and produce monetary consequences.

BRITTAN—I very much agree with David Laidler's view of what some of us miscall the 'natural level of unemployment', and how to reduce it. The besetting sin of post-war politics is the belief that you determine a desirable level of unemployment and ask the Treasury to manipulate the levers. Therefore I think that the gulf between our thinking here and orthodox establishment thought is still a little larger than Peter Jay was supposing. But I have certainly, in what I have said myself on housing, taken the view that measures such as council house subsidies, rent controls, measures taken by woolly-minded governments under populist pressure, do increase the natural rate of unemployment. So-called housing policies, whether Margaret Thatcher's or Anthony Crosland's, do increase the natural rate of unemployment.

Somebody earlier asked a question of fact. Are governments terrified of sit-ins, are they terrified of the increased transitional unemployment involved in moving from our present frightening rate of inflation to something a little lower? The answer to both these questions is 'yes'. Mainstream leadership in the Conservative and Labour Parties is absolutely terrified of these manifestations. And I think the so-called concession in the Conservative manifesto saying that monetary policy is important is worthless if it is taken in conjunction with remarks that the Party will not tolerate an increase in unemployment. What that means is that as soon as unemployment starts rising, in the Upper Clyde or elsewhere, politicians are going to tell officials: 'We have got to get it down.' And bang goes the money supply policy.

GEORGE SCHWARTZ[5]—We shall certainly be told by Professor Friedman that the real power of trade unions lies in the restriction on entry. Now woolly-minded governments have laid down the principle of equal opportunity for women. If that principle is implemented, there is going to be some fun and games in the economy. Can anyone tell me what jobs there are in the economy today which cannot be performed by women? The primacy of the brawny arm which does all the hard work of the world has gone and now we've got to the stage of the delicate fingers. Now what jobs are there— some of you must have a daughter of that age—what jobs are there

---

[5] Formerly of the London School of Economics and the *Sunday Times*.

that she can not do that men can do? Can she drive a train on London Transport? If there had been a trade union of Channel swimmers, no woman would have been able to swim the Channel. And it would have been proved that no woman ought to be allowed to swim the Channel.

The Chairman could tell you what operates in the printing industry. The linotype is operated like typing, it was a mistake of the printing unions not to class typing as printing, saying this is exclusively a man's job. Then we should have heard all the bunk about typing being bad for women, bad for expectant mothers because it cramps the womb when you sit down and type. You might say coalmining is a special case, but we know what happens when you make anything a special case. If you go into a steel works you do not see men standing and sweating over a furnace: you see somebody pressing keys. Once we get to the stage when women can really infiltrate into every occupation, the great power of the unions will disappear.

MILTON FRIEDMAN—I would like this afternoon to answer the very thoughtful and provoking questions raised this morning, so let me make only a few preliminary comments.

I felt Mr Jay's discussion of the problem was extremely illuminating in separating out issues. What he has properly described as a Hayekian position is what I would be inclined to call a Haberlerian position—also Austrian in origin, but I think it is Professor Haberler who has been most consistent in maintaining the kind of position you have described.

LORD ROBBINS—Without being chauvinistic, may I ask you to remember A. C. Pigou who was pushed around a good deal in the pre-war controversy. After the war he wrote a little book called *Lapses from Full Employment*, in which he sufficiently intimated that, while of course he was not recommending lowering wages in the depressed areas to cure unemployment, he yet thought there might be some slight danger of lapses from full employment if wages were pushed above what he considered to be the equilibrium point. So you must call it the Pigovian/Hayekian/Haberlerian point of view.

FRIEDMAN—Since it is a point of view with which I shall differ I am not sure that I am rendering homage to Mr Pigou by including him in that group. I think the issue is much more than semantic. I do not really believe it is a semantic issue at all. I wish it were true that we are all in agreement but are only using different words.

But we are not. I believe it is very important to separate out the analytical problem from the practical and empirical problem. And I believe that what is wrong with the view that you described as one of woolly government is woolly thinking. That is what I want to try to explain.

In the first place, Mr Jay said that in conditions in which you have a commitment to full employment, and in which you have trade unions, such and such will follow. Now is it a semantic distinction to say that only the first of those conditions is relevant? I do not think so. The essence of the kind of analytical apparatus that we have been building up these past years is this: suppose you have a world in which, in technical language, the long-run Phillips curve[6] is vertical—that's really the key analytical issue. If so, you can talk about a natural rate of unemployment, and you are in exactly the position with respect to the problem of stable employment that Wicksell analysed so well with respect to the problem of an interest rate. He pointed out, and I think it is widely accepted everywhere today, that a monetary policy which sought to fix a nominal interest rate *above* the natural rate would be unstable. And a monetary policy which sought to fix the interest rate *below* the natural rate would be unstable. A monetary policy which sought to fix it at the natural rate, if by some magic it could be defined, would be meta-stable, that is, it would not have any determinate equilibrium position but would move with the wind.

Exactly the same propositions apply if a government commits itself to a full employment target. If that target is below the natural rate, then the situation is unstable. And anything that comes along to disturb it will cause it to move away. It might on one occasion be the creation of a few trade unions that causes it to move away; it might on another occasion be council houses. It might be a change in the terms of trade, it might be the loss of an export industry. There is a sense in which you can say in each of these cases that 'the cause' of the inflation in the first instance was a strong trade union, 'the cause' of the inflation in the second instance was council houses, and 'the cause' of the inflation in the third instance was a trade deficit. But surely it is analytically cleaner to say that the fundamental cause of the inflation in all of these cases is the adoption of a de-stabilising monetary policy, namely of an

---

[6] Milton Friedman, *How Stands the Phillips Curve?*, IEA Occasional Paper (early 1975).

attempt to use a monetary weapon to fix something which it cannot fix. So that in that sense there is much more than a semantic issue.

That is one analytical observation. Now I want to go to a second. Suppose there is a non-vertical Phillips curve. Suppose we are wrong: suppose the Keynesian analysis is correct. It will still not follow analytically that under those assumptions strong trade unions are a cause of inflation. First of all, you have to distinguish between strong and stronger. It is the *change* from one degree of strength to another that has an effect. If unions are strong and have been strong, they have long since done their work. Their relative wages are high, other relative wages are low. At this level the belief that strong unions produce inflation is completely an analytical confusion between relative effects and general effects. It is the confusion that has been promoted in other areas where it is easier to see: for example, supposing that a world in which all industries are monopolistic would have a lower rate of utilisation of capacity than a world in which you had perfect competition. There is no reason to expect that at all. It incorporates an invalid generalisation: from one monopoly in a competitive world to a world of monopolies. Suppose you take the industrial case of monopolies which demonstrates the analytical point with fewer emotional overtones, so that it is easier to state. In such a world if there is only one monopolistic industry it would produce a lower level of output than a purely competitive industry would produce. Does it follow that in a world of monopolies total output would be less, that total use of resources would be less? No—output would be distorted, the division of output among various branches of industry would be different than it otherwise would be. But what would happen? Some enterprises would have stronger monopoly positions than others, and the strong monopoly industries would be producing at a lower level of output than they would under a purely competitive situation. And the weaker monopolies would be producing at a higher level of output than they otherwise would.

Now it is interesting that Haberler explicitly accepts this analysis for business enterprises. He agrees completely that in business a given level of monopoly power will not produce inflation. He agrees that an increase in monopoly power will produce a transitory problem in which one industry will expand its price, which will cause people there to be unemployed. There may be a transitory period during which unemployment is frictional but sooner or later relative prices elsewhere will go down. However, he asserts, that analysis does not apply to trade unions. And it is at this point that the woolliness enters. I have never seen an analytically satisfactory distinction between the argument for trade unions and the argument for industrial concerns. It is said that industrial concerns maximise profits, trade unions do not. This argument is irrelevant. The only question is: is there something which trade union leaders maximise? Is there an equilibrium level of real wages? If there is, the analysis that is applied to industry also applies to labour.

Let me be very much more specific and explain what I mean when I say that, if I were to accept the straight Keynesian argument, you would still not be able to come out with the conclusion about trade unions. Let us suppose hypothetically we have a great increase in the power of some trade unions. That means they are able to raise their relative wages, and fewer people will be employed in the industry. There will be more people to be employed elsewhere, and there will be unemployment. Now let us assume with the Keynesians that you can eliminate the unemployment by expansionary measures. That is a once-for-all effect. It is not a *continuing* process of inflation, because thereafter, as David Laidler properly said, the now stronger union will simply keep pace with the inflation. It will not generate any more unemployment, and therefore you simply have to follow the Keynesian policy of reducing real wages elsewhere by the indirect process of inflation. You would then absorb the extra unemployed. Once you had done that you could stay there—there would no longer be inflation. So that even if you accept the Keynesian analysis, trade unions are not a source of continuing inflation.

Escalator clauses

Entirely aside from Mr Gordon Pepper's question whether you ought to have escalator clauses or not, thinking of a world in which you have universal escalator clauses is an enormously effective way to clear your mind about the misconceptions. I ask you to turn over in your minds the analysis of a purely hypothetical world. Consider a hypothetical world in which everybody is unionised —I do not even want to go into the case where you have got 50/50 because I am not sure it is really a better case. I think that all the phenomena which are attributed to trade unions can be found where there are no trade unions at all. Fundamentally, two speakers gave the right relation between inflation and trade unions. Mr John

Flemming and Mr Richard Henderson both pointed out that the relationship was that inflation strengthens trade unions, not that strong trade unions produce inflation. I am sure that is an empirically correct analysis because inflation means you have to have frequent changes in money wage rates. If there are trade unions those changes come through them and they appear to be the instrument of improving the lot of their members. If there are no trade unions the adjustments in money wages come through the market; they are not attributed to any individual. Nobody knows who does it. So I believe that inflation does have a very important role in strengthening trade unions, not the other way round.

But consider the pure analytical case. Suppose a world in which trade unions enter into contracts on a three-year basis. Some of the contracts expire this week, some the next. It will simplify the analysis not to suppose them all to expire at once, although it does not alter the essence. Every such contract provides for 100 per cent indexation. Now I ask you to construct any plausible analysis whereby conflicts among those trade unions on *real* wage terms (nobody is bargaining in terms of money wages at all) can lead to inflation? How do they lead, by any device you can conceive, to a pressure for money wages to rise more rapidly than productivity?

This way of putting it reveals the fundamental issue that underlies all this concern about trade unions. Mr Brittan has called my attention to a sentence I wrote in my Paper on *Monetary Correction*[7] published by this excellent organisation, the Institute of Economic Affairs, which is sponsoring today's seminar. In the Paper I said that one of the arguments made about escalator clauses (I believe the argument which really underlies the stress on trade union matters) is that escalator clauses would prevent inflation from resolving inconsistent demands of workers which add up more than 100 per cent of real income (that is the kind of analysis made); and it is argued that workers who would accept a lower real wage produced by unanticipated inflation will not be willing to accept the same real wage in explicit negotiations.

So the real argument about inflation—'do trade unions matter?'—is really that you can fool trade unions and their workers to do something implicitly which they will not be willing to do explicitly. What I said in the Paper was: 'If this view is correct on a wide enough

---

[7] Occasional Paper 41, IEA, 1974, pp. 31-32.

scale to be important, I see no ultimate outcome than either runaway inflation or an authoritarian society ruled by force.' That is an overstatement because even runaway inflation is not a solution to the problem. If you have an irreconcilable conflict of that kind it really has nothing to do with inflation but with whether you have a stable society or are going to convert economic conflict into violent political conflict. I do not believe that is your situation, nor our situation in the USA. But yet I believe it is that conception that underlies the insistence of economists like Haberler and others that trade unions produce inflation.

PETER JAY—The discussion has been very helpful to me, at least so far as most of the contributions are concerned. The key question between Professor Laidler and me, indeed between Friedmanites and Hayekians, is not whether or not unions can raise the general pay level when the money supply is not rising—we both agree that they cannot—but whether or not, if they try to, they can cause unemployment. It still seems to me that it is perfectly easy to see how they might in that situation; and I think the passage which Professor Friedman has just quoted, instigated by Sam Brittan, comes to the absolute nub of the matter. That is exactly what those of us who think as I do believe is happening. If Professor Friedman says, 'Oh well, that doesn't really count, because that just means society is not viable', it scarcely meets our point, because it is exactly the conclusion we are drawing.

The point is exactly this: that if 100 per cent of the people, to take an extreme case, refuse to work unless they are paid the equivalent of 105 per cent of the value of what they produce, or indeed 150 per cent, what will happen is that nobody will work. If in that situation the government intercedes to maintain full employment or indeed any level of employment at all, whether or not it is woolly-minded, then you will get exactly what we fear: inflation accelerating to an infinite rate with grave political and social consequences. It is as if all workers belonged to one union which refused to allow its members to work for less than an indexed wage worth 105 per cent of the weekly product of each worker; and all employment was with the central bank (or other money-printing authority). That is the view of myself —and I think of Sam Brittan, but he will speak for himself—and of others about what is in fact happening in our society.

Professor Friedman says that is not what is happening. I think I agree with him, for what that's worth, that it is not happening in the

United States. Nor is it likely to happen in the United States. But I think it is happening here. I think it is equally happening—some countries are a little further down the same road, some are not so far down this road—in most of the Western European countries. That is why it is such a serious matter and why it has become important to persuade people not to insist on being paid 105 per cent or 150 per cent of the value of what they are producing. If that is what incomes policy is about, and if that is what is at issue, it does seem to me that an incomes policy, whether or not it has the side-effect of making trade unions stronger, is an important matter in our present-day economy.

4. The Crisis — When and Why Did it Start?

Professor of Economics,
University of Manchester

THE AUTHOR

DAVID E. W. LAIDLER was born in 1938 and educated at the London School of Economics, where he graduated BSc Econ with First Class Honours in 1959; the University of Syracuse (MA Economics, 1960); and the University of Chicago (PhD, 1964). He has taught in both Britain (LSE, 1961-62; Lecturer in Economics, University of Essex, 1966-69) and the USA (Acting Professor, University of California, Berkeley, 1963-66; Acting Assistant Professor, Stanford University, Autumn 1964). He was appointed Professor of Economics at the University of Manchester in 1969. In 1971 he organised the History of Economic Thought Conference held at the University of Manchester to commemorate the centenary of the publication of W. S. Jevons's *Theory of Political Economy*; and he was the British Association for the Advancement of Science Lister Lecturer for 1972.

His publications include *The Demand for Money—Theories and Evidence* (International Textbook Co., 1969), and *Introduction to Microeconomics* (Philip Allan Publishers, 1974), and he edited (with David Purdy) *Labour Markets and Inflation* (Manchester University Press, 1974).

I would like to concentrate on the question 'why' rather than the question 'when' because I think that is the much more interesting problem as far as the current crisis is concerned.

At the moment, as everybody here knows, we have a rate of inflation which, depending upon quite how you measure it, and over what time-period, is running at somewhere between 17 and 20 per cent; and a rate of inflation which is widely expected to accelerate, for the next 6 or 8 months at least. We also have a situation in which industry is complaining loudly about liquidity, bankruptcies are beginning to appear on a fairly spectacular scale and are expected to continue. The unemployment rate is beginning to creep up and it is widely forecast that figures not far short of a million ought to turn up in 1975.

Now these figures are not very pleasant, but if you would compare them to the data generated by what were called crises in the past, the 1920s and 1930s, though they are uncomfortable you would not really rate them for the title. I think that there is a crisis, however. It is really a crisis in English economics. I shall argue today that our current mess is the predictable consequence of applying bad economics to a tractable situation. Unfortunately the practitioners of bad economics appear to have drawn a lesson from recent experience that their bad economics was good economics. And there is every likelihood that that bad economics is going to be applied again.

That is the 'why' of the crisis. The answer to the 'when' is a trivial matter. I hope it will emerge from what I have to say that somewhere round about 1971 and 1972 was when we began to get into trouble.

Post-war British inflation

A brief history of post-war inflation in Britain: If you start with the Korean war the inflation rate fell cyclically but steadily until round about 1960, when it levelled off, and began to accelerate slowly in about 1966-67. The rate of acceleration of the inflation rate has been going up ever since with the exception of 1971-72. Those are the basic facts we have to explain.

I don't want to go back over the history of the 1950s and early 1960s, but I would argue that the inflation we are now living with began from two causes. First, we were operating a fixed exchange rate *vis à vis* the rest of the world in the mid-1960s when the United States finally gave up what I would regard as sensible fiscal and monetary policies, and went into deficit financing of war expenditure on a large scale. That produced an inflation right across the world which was linked to the United States via fixed exchange rates, an inflation that the rest of the world chose to import rather than let their exchange rates vary. I do not want to blame the United States for our problems—we chose to import their inflation by maintaining a fixed exchange rate. Indeed we exacerbated that problem a little bit in the short run by the devaluation of 1967 which was bound to give a once-and-for-all kick to the British price level. That is what got us going.

In 1969-70 we had a pretty severe monetary contraction in this country. This was partly the result of following the instructions of the IMF and partly something we again imported through the structure of fixed exchange rates from the United States which was also having a monetary contraction about that time. I don't want to try and attribute portions of blame here to these two causes.

For a while that monetary contraction appeared to produce no effects whatsoever. I can certainly recall lots of newspaper articles at the time saying: 'What is this about monetarism? Look at what's happening to the inflation rate, to unemployment, to the money supply, the predicted relationships simple aren't there'. Of course the relationships were there; everybody who had studied those relationships with any care at all knew that there were time-lags involved in the relationships. And, sure enough, somewhere round 1970-71 we began to get unemployment; but of course the inflation that had previously been generated was going on. It even accelerated temporarily in the face of rising unemployment.

It was then announced that this demonstrated that the market economy no longer worked. 'Here is rising unemployment *and* rising inflation; these two things are incompatible with orthodox market economics. The world has changed.' The fact that the inflation rate began to fall in the winter of 1971 and came near to halving in 12 months by the end of 1972 either went unnoticed or was attributed to a fortunate falling off in the rate of inflation of world food prices. This is *describing* what happened to the price index rather than *explaining* what happened. Notice the story I am telling—a monetary contraction which had its predictable effect, spread out over a two-year period. This evidence was grossly misinterpreted by what passed for informed opinion in this country at the time, with the unfortunate results with which we are now living. We had the Barber budget of 1972: the policy of 'going-for-growth' at any cost. The intellectual underpinnings of that policy were that you could do anything you liked to aggregate demand and it was not going to affect inflation because the market economy had stopped working.

'Going-for-growth'

It suddenly became apparent that 'going-for-growth' was not quite working out properly either, so we had what Professor Robbins called prices and incomes policy this morning. To digress for a moment: he taught me monetary economics; he was the first to mention the quantity of money in my presence . . . being unfashionable economics at the time it was taught under the guise of the history of economic thought, rather in the way Marxist economics is now taught. He taught me something about the precise use of language in economics. Those are not prices and incomes *policies,* they are wage and price *controls.* I think we confuse an enormous number of issues if we forget that.

Inflation was allegedly to be brought under control by undertaking a policy of wage and price controls, modelled on the American pattern, which was widely publicised again by informed opinion in this country as being a roaring success. We know what happened! That takes us roughly to the end of 1973. There is some difficulty about working out exactly where we are now. My view is that towards the end of 1973 the combination of the winter budget and the modifications to banking regulations and what have you set in motion a really fierce monetary contraction relative to trend. I should explain why I think that, because it is very much a minority opinion, though perhaps less so now than six months ago.

Monetary contraction

Monetary contractions do not do much unless they continue for about a year. That seems to be the lesson of recent monetary history. It takes about 12 months for them to work through. Moreover when sharp changes in monetary affairs are taking place, the monetary indicators—the M1s and the M2s and the M3s—sometimes diverge. But roughly speaking over the last 12 months M1 has either not grown at all or fallen slightly after having grown at an annual rate of something like 14 or 15 per cent over the previous two years. The rate of expansion of M3 has come down from about 28 per cent or so to an order of magnitude of about 15 per cent. I have heard arguments about excess liquidity in the system and all the rest of it. Perhaps there is an element of truth in it, but I don't believe that you can explain contractions of that order of magnitude, sustained now over 12 months, simply as technical adjustments to excess liquidity. And I think the liquidity problems we are now seeing in industry, the bankruptcies and the rising unemployment level, are the results of monetary policy. I think we are now well into the throes of the next downturn.

The question is: how are we going to handle that next downturn? That depends upon the lessons that have been drawn from recent experiences. The lessons I draw are that monetary policy was at fault. The policy implied is a *gradual* contraction of the rate of monetary expansion bolstered by indexing. We should really take a long time about carrying out such a policy.

The lessons that appear to have been drawn, however, by those who make up at least a section of informed opinion seem to be quite different. And they seem to me to be based on downright bad economics for which there is becoming increasingly less excuse.

The inflation of the last few years is blamed on two things: first, the activities of aggressive trade unions, and, secondly, the unfortunate behaviour of world prices, in particular world commodity prices, combined with the unfortunate behaviour of the British exchange rate. I have heard it argued only a couple of weeks ago that really the last set of wage and price controls were very successful, because they held domestically-generated inflation down to an incredibly low level; everything else was just awfully unfortunate. So let us examine these two arguments and see how much water they hold.

We have talked about trade unions at some length this morning. Let me summarise what I said. The argument about trade union aggressiveness is bad economics. To start with, it confuses relative prices with the absolute price level. Moreover there is not a shred of empirical evidence in its favour, and it's always comforting to have good economics confirmed by empirical evidence. The argument about commodity prices, and world prices in general, is in essence very similar to the trade union argument. It too confuses cause with effect; it confuses relative prices with absolute prices.

I argued this morning that if one union bid up its wages, that was going to change the structure of relative wages and unless something was being done on the monetary side it was not going to affect the absolute price level. So also, if imported commodity prices go up, if the terms of trade turn against a country, that country is certainly going to be poorer, there is no doubt about that. The output which is particularly intensive in the use of imported commodities is going to rise in price relative to other commodities. But that is no reason to expect the *general* price level to increase—it is every reason to expect the structure of relative prices to change.

That is what would happen if you had a fixed exchange rate and if the increase in commodity prices was independent of anything that might be going on in the monetary sector. Oil is to some extent a case in point. But I would put two points quite simply. When you have inflation going and when people begin to *expect* inflation to continue, they begin to move out of money into real stores of value. You can buy commodities on margin; therefore it is particularly easy to get out of money into commodites. To some extent —I do not know to what extent—the rise in commodity prices, far from being a *cause* of inflation, is a *predictable effect*. Along with that you must recognise that real expansion was going on in the early stages of the present inflation right across the industrialised world and was putting pressure on commodity prices. Again, the rise in commodity prices was a consequence of monetary expansion and not an independent contributory factor to rising prices.

Finally, we come to the exchange rate. The exchange rate fell and drove up the sterling price of imports. The reason why the exchange rate fell is that sterling was being created at such a rate that it could not maintain its market value. And, again, far from being a cause of domestic inflation, that fall in the exchange rate was a consequence of domestically-generated inflation. Indeed we can go even further. Suppose with a given rate of monetary expansion you institute a set of wage and price controls on domestic output, and suppose you are successful. What will happen? To the extent that domestic prices cannot rise to absorb domestic purchasing power, it is going to spill over into the import sector, drive down the exchange rate and change the structure of relative prices. But of course there's going to be no overall effect on the rate of inflation. You are going to get the same *average* rate of inflation with a changed structure of *relative* prices as a result of directly controlling domestic prices.

No one should be surprised at that. If you confuse relative prices with absolute prices, and institute a policy which might do something about relative prices but cannot do anything about absolute prices, you should not be surprised to find that such a policy did indeed change relative prices without affecting the absolute price level.

Nevertheless arguments about unions and world prices are still widely accepted. I don't know why; there is no evidence why they should be. There is no serious economic analysis that says they should be. But nevertheless they are accepted. I am beginning to despair as an academic economist of discovering how to get through to people on these matters.

The frustration hypothesis

What of this business of frustration, of claims adding up to 105 per cent of income and society breaking down because of fundamental conflicts? I have no doubt that those tendencies exist in our society now, but again I would argue that they are the result of inflation and not a cause of it. If you continually promise people money wage increases, which they initially read as being real wage increases, but when they spend the money wages they find are not real wage increases, they are going to say: 'You led me to believe I could have a higher real income and I have been deceived.' And of course everybody is going to be very frustrated. They have been misled and they're going to ask for 105 per cent because they have been told they can have 105 per cent. It takes them time to learn that they cannot. In the interim you get all the social disruption, the strikes, etc. that are the predictable and universal consequences of every inflation. There is nothing unique about recent experience. But these are consequences; they are in no way causes.

What is going to happen? Why is there going to be—why have we got—a crisis? I think we have a crisis because, if I read the next two years correctly, they are going to be a repeat performance of 1971 and 1972 with bigger numbers. The inflation rate is going to be higher, and the unemployment rate is going to be higher. How much higher I am not prepared to say, because we are extrapolating far beyond the bounds of post-war experience. And it really is not possible to be sure about anything in such circumstances.

One thing I will extrapolate from recent experience is the likely behaviour of the authorities. They are going to conclude that they can do something about the unemployment. They are going once again to fall victim to what I think now must be the most dangerous half-truth in the history of economic thought, which is that Keynes taught us we could have any level of unemployment simply by manipulating aggregate demand. That is true—in the short run we can—but, as Milton Friedman said this morning, if you want to have any level of unemployment you like with a given structure of labour markets and demographic structure of the population, you are going to have either continually accelerating or continually decelerating inflation. Unfortunately the authorities do not seem to understand.

I read in the *Sunday Times*[1] only the other day, for the 98th time it must be, that the experience of 1969-1972 shows that monetarist policy prescriptions do not work. Those years demonstrably show exactly the opposite. I read in the *Economist* last week that Sir Keith Joseph is confused because he does not seem to understand that inflation is a matter of excess demand and unemployment is a matter of excess supply and we have both and this is puzzling. It is not puzzling and it was not puzzling to anybody who had read the academic literature on inflation written in the mid-1960s. No one should have been puzzled in 1969-72. All the theory was worked out before the present experience—ready and waiting for it. Monetarist theories are not *ex post* rationalisations and I think it is important to get that straight.

More inflation to come

Nevertheless I am afraid we are going to have yet another expansion this autumn. If we do, by Christmas 1975 things will be looking up. The inflation rate will still be coming down as a result of what is happening now, the unemployment rate will be beginning to come down as a result of what has been done then. Everybody will be cheering and saying: 'You see, the market economy does not work and the monetarists were wrong—and look how wonderful things are.' But wait till you see the inflation rate we shall get out of this in 1976-77! And then I think the cycle will start all over again.

Milton Friedman knows more than I do about the monetary history of various inflations. But this is the classic approach to

---

[1] 'Inflation: they're all agin it', *Sunday Times,* 15 September, 1974.

ultimate hyper-inflation. This is how it starts. Hyper-inflations get publicised as things that happen very quickly—you know, over a couple of years. But that is the end of them. They build up very slowly over time through stop-go cycles like this until eventually one cycle gets too big to handle. I do not know how many cycles we are away from ultimate ruin at the moment in this country. I suspect two or three. But we are close enough now that I think we ought to be feeling uncomfortable.

Good and bad economics

There is nothing inevitable about getting there provided we apply good economics as opposed to bad economics. Let me finish on that note. I do not think it is right to present the debate about economic policy in this country between two schools of thought, one called monetarist and one called Keynesian—although Keynes must be turning in his grave about that!—with equal claim to respect for the intellectual coherence of their views and the amount of evidence they can marshall on their side. That might have been right, and probably was right, perhaps 15 years ago. But it is quite simply no longer the case. By any standards of evidence in social science (even if those standards of evidence are often weak), there is far more evidence on the monetarists' side than there is on the Keynesian side.

Monetarists are continually being asked by Keynesian economists to provide an account of the transmission mechanism for the relationship between money and prices. We have continually been responding for 15 years. But they still come back five minutes later and say: 'You have not given an account of the transmission mechanism.' And, we are told, correlation is no evidence of causation. We know that. But when it comes to trade union militancy, or the efficacy of wage and price controls, there is not even correlation, let alone an account of the mechanism of causation. And yet I fear we shall soon be asked to swallow another dose of policy based on—I repeat—bad economics and no empirical evidence.

DISCUSSION

LORD ROBBINS—I think that I am going to depart just a little from the printed programme. We are billed at 2.45 to release Professor Friedman to your attacks. But I think before that release

I am going to ask to have about a quarter of an hour of questions on what Professor Laidler has said. Professor Friedman has just suggested to me that if there are, in this rather tough and courageous group, timid souls who do not want to stand on their feet but who yet would like to dispute in one way or another, if they would send up written questions, Professor Friedman is prepared to read them.

I happen to agree with 90 per cent of what Laidler said and I am not going to ask him any questions, but I am sure that there is somebody who does not agree with 90 per cent.

JOHN FLEMMING—I too agree with at least 90 per cent of what David Laidler has said, but let me again try to muddy the waters a little with some qualifications. Particularly I would like to take up the deterioriation in Britain's terms of trade.

This is really rather important in the problem that we now have to face. It is a large part of the reason why we have to try to bring down the real wages of people (other than academics!) over the fairly short future. It seems to me that there is some connection between this issue and inflation; and a moderately woolly-minded, or even soft-hearted, government might be justified possibly in allowing a once-and-for-all—admittedly only once-and-for-all—increase in the price level in response to a discrete deterioration in the country's terms of trade such as has occurred within the last 12 months, if you will allow such a government not to have anticipated such a change. It seems to me perfectly reasonable that the frictions in the economy and the asymmetries between the effects of excess supplies and excess demands should be such that, in the process of adjustment to a change in the terms of trade, changes in relative prices and relative wages within the economy, a certain amount of unemployment might be expected to emerge if one were to stick rigidly to a policy consistent with price stability. Under those circumstances it might be worthwhile taking advantage of the short-run trade-off between the rate of change of prices and levels of unemployment in order to cushion the blow, to spread the costs—the costs of adjustment—over some period, and allow some rise in the price level and therefore temporarily to have some level of inflation.

LAIDLER—I quite agree with everything John Flemming has said. He said that the government might be wise to permit a temporary inflation in order to help us over these frictions. It *might* be wise and it would have to *permit* it. But what has been suggested is that the

61

poor old government has had no choice but to suffer the inflationary consequences of an oil price increase wished on us by the Arabs. And that is really the kind of reasoning which I am attacking. If you want to see some empirical evidence, consider that Germans import oil, Dutchmen import oil—and would it not be lovely if we had their rates of inflation?

J. R. SARGENT[1]—I would like to take up part of David Laidler's historical survey and link it to the point he was making this morning that it was not possible for any trade union to use monopolistic power to raise the general level of money wages. Supposing that one could show that on some morning all trade unionists and all employees with a bargaining position woke up and suddenly decided that they were going to go for an increase in money wages, so that you had the sort of across-the-board increase of money wages which economists are used to proposing to their students in Keynesian models. Then it seems to me that you could put the economy into the sort of dilemma which Peter Jay was outlining, where the government either had to accept unemployment in order to fight inflation, or inflation in order to fight unemployment. It seems to me that, if you could demonstrate the possibility of the reasonableness of this sort of behaviour occurring, you would be in his kind of model.

The question is whether you can demonstrate that it is reasonable for this sort of thing to occur. I think that in the years he was referring to, 1969-70, there was a particular phenomenon which may have explained why at that time there might have been a sudden once-for-all across-the-board increase in money wages. That is to say that over this period it can be shown that the rate of growth of personal real disposable income was at a very slow rate, not simply in relation to rates which people had got used to in the past but also in relation to the rate of growth of the Gross National Product in real terms per head, so that out of what people were producing they were getting a diminishing proportion. I think one can show this to have been the case over that period, and that it may have constituted a reason why there should have been a sudden upsurge in money wages, which one would interpret presumably, not by saying it was simply the trade unions that did it, but that the trade unions did it because they were in some sense provoked.

---

[1] Group Economic Adviser, Midland Bank, formerly Professor of Economics, University of Warwick.

If that were the case, what is the reason why there was the development of this sudden slackening in the growth of disposable income in relation to national product per head? I think that what we had at that time was—on top of a tendency for non-consumption claims on the national income to rise, both through the rise in public expenditure and through the rise in the share of investment—also a sudden additional inroad on consumption forced by the very large balance of payments and the Jenkins budget which made a final drastic attempt to get rid of it. This of course also explains, as a result of this large budget surplus, the severe money squeeze which Professor Laidler mentioned. But I would submit that there is this possible original cause why there might have been an across-the-board upsurge of money wages at that time which could have put us into the sort of dilemma Peter Jay was outlining.

LAIDLER—There are two points really here. One is the general point and the other is the interpretation of a particular piece of economic history.

Now it is certainly true in any kind of macro-economic model that if you bring in as a *deus ex machina* an increase in the level of money wages and nothing else happens you get unemployment. That is a well-known analytical result: unemployment which can be dissipated by allowing the money supply to increase. It is an equally well-known property of the same macro-economic model that, if you have a sudden fall in liquidity preference, you will have a rise in the price level without any monetary expansion. And that if you have continuously falling liquidity preference you will have a continuous inflation without any increase in money supply. So there is no disagreement about what is logically possible in the structure of a macro-economic model.

Where there might be disagreement between us is on whether the kind of behaviour that Professor Sargent postulates would be maximising behaviour in any sense on the part of the trade union, just as there would be a question whether a sudden fall in liquidity preference could be the consequence of maximising behaviour by individuals. Now I daresay you can construct models in which it would be, and in which it would not be.

So now we come to the empirical evidence. Has it ever happened? All I can say is that on the best evidence put, not by monetarists, but by Keynesians, it has not. And I should just say one thing: it is not my work but the work of my colleagues David Purdy and George

Zis, that has gone into this matter very, very thoroughly.[2] In 1969-70 there was a wage explosion. But there was also really very expansionary monetary policy from 1966 right through to 1969, which of course is the main reason why the devaluation did not work. There is a lovely paper by Kierskowski and Jonson from the LSE, sub-titled 'How the British invented the J curve',[3] simply pointing out that you can explain this delay in terms of monetary expansion. The monetary expansion of course was the result of the monetary authorities, or let's just say the authorities, being too chicken-hearted to remind the labour force that devaluation meant a fall in real income. So they were putting off the evil day.

Price inflation began to take care of the levels of real income, and of course by 1969-70 trade unionists and non-trade unionists alike were getting frustrated and put in a push for higher money wages. That is *part* of the on-going inflationary process. It is in no sense a *cause* of it. To conclude: Peter Oppenheimer last night, when debating with Milton Friedman,[4] said 'On this side of the panel[5] we think that inflation is a very complicated process'. Unfortunately I was not allowed to get in from the audience with a response, so I shall make it now. Yes indeed, inflation is a very complicated process, and on this side of the debate we do not pretend to understand all about the process. What we do argue is that the *cause* of inflation really is very simple: it is monetary expansion.

FRIEDMAN—May I make one comment? On a purely logical level, I believe that Professor Sargent's supposition is not sufficient. His supposition is—has to be—suppose that on some morning all employees in unions and non-unions decided they were not going to work unless they got a higher monetary wage. But suppose also that this was a purely temporary aberration that would pass away

---

[2] 'Trade Unions and Inflation: A Reappraisal of the Evidence', in D. Laidler and D. Purdy (eds.), *Inflation and Labour Markets*, Manchester University Press, 1974.

[3] P. D. Jonson and H. I. Kierskowski, 'The Balance of Payments, an Analytical Exercise', LSE Mimeo, April 1974.

[4] BBC-2 *Controversy* debate, televised on 23 September, 1974.

[5] The members of the panel were: R. R. Neild, Professor of Economics, University of Cambridge; Peter Oppenheimer, Senior Tutor in Economics, University of Oxford; Geoffrey Maynard, Professor of Economics, University of Reading; and G. D. N. Worswick, Director of the National Institute of Economic and Social Research.

within two days. Because unless you add that supposition you do not have a source of *inflation*—you have a source of an *explosion*. The implicit assumption that the government has this dilemma is that the government will be able to take away from all employees what you assume they were interested in getting without their reacting to it. If, for good reasons, for bad reasons, or for indifferent reasons, they firmly decided that they were not going to work unless they got a higher money wage at current price levels, and if they are not fools, which they are not, they would recognise that there was no difference in principle between a 10 per cent rise in prices and a 10 per cent decline in real wages. Then, of course, they do not hand the government a dilemma; they establish a situation in which you explode. So I think you have to append to your hypothesis that it is a purely temporary aberration that will pass off as soon as they have had a good night's sleep, and that once they've had a good night's sleep the government can take away from them what it gave them today.

LORD ROBBINS—You don't admit the possibility of slow explosion?

FRIEDMAN—Of course: explosions can take some time, and you may be saying that you are still in the process of that explosion. I am only saying that it does not alter the particular dilemma. The dilemma that is posed to the government is not the dilemma between somehow or other maintaining indefinitely a higher level of inflation or a higher level of unemployment. If there is a dilemma for the government it is: how *fast* shall we let this explosion take place?

LORD ROBBINS—Any more questions before Professor Milton Friedman is fully deployed?

PROFESSOR A. J. MERRETT[6]—My interest is from the standpoint of corporate profitability and finance. I would welcome some enlightenment on the question whether historical experience about the effects of inflation could not be modified by a new factor having been introduced which you might call the 'self-destruct factor'. Governments can build in negative productivity in industry by a simple process of imposing price controls and operating a tax system based upon historical costs, thus creating a liquidity problem in

---

[6] Professor of Corporate Finance at the London Graduate School of Business Studies.

companies which forces them into diminished productivity of various kinds, short-run expedients to try to maintain their liquidity. Is it perhaps the case that this particular factor in the UK could be significant in creating an almost automatic self-destruct mechanism that increases the rate of inflation by diminishing the rate of productivity?

LAIDLER—Very briefly, I think the answer has to be 'yes'. These tendencies are present and they are a special case of what you always get in inflationary situations, namely uncertainty about the meaning of the value of money, and uncertainty about the future course of the value of money, which leads to *ex-post*-non-maximising decisions being taken. And the current tax structure, which is not indexed, along with depreciation rules and such must be having this effect.

But there is a much simpler destructive mechanism in inflation which I think must be present in all rapid inflations. It is that while they are getting under way you have what are effectively negative real rates of interest, which makes it privately profitable to destroy wealth. And you should not be surprised to find that that is what happens.

QUESTIONER—On making the monetary prescription acceptable, much of what Milton Friedman has been saying about indexing is really in the interests of this policy. A further point is whether it would be possible to take a lot of the agony out of the transition period by offering the unemployed a larger amount of unemployment pay. Maybe you would have to add to it something like taxing social benefits in order to erase the anomaly of people being better off out of work than in work. But, given that sort of package, to what extent could one run it and make a public announcement: we're going to run it for two years or until the vacancies start rising. That sort of announcement would be advertising to people that you believe this is the way the situation works. You do not wish to punish the poor people in the community. Why not talk about it in that way? But to what extent is it feasible to have this trade-off without undermining the monetary policy?

LAIDLER—I cannot give any numerical answer to that kind of question, but I think the following point is worth making. If you make it less painful to be unemployed, you will have more people on the margin choosing to stay unemployed a little longer until they find the job they want. That is to say, you will increase the natural rate of unemployment. And that is to say, in turn, that to get a given slow-down in the rate of inflation over a given period, the more comfortable it is to be unemployed the higher the level of measured unemployment you are going to have. The mechanism whereby unemployment brings the inflation rate down is a very cruel mechanism. It is a mechanism of hurting people and persuading them that they are better off accepting a lower wage than they thought they could get rather than stay unemployed. And you have to do that or you do not get them to accept that lower wage. I do not think that we monetarists would do anyone a service by pretending that our policies would be painless.

QUESTIONER—It seems to me that possibly firms may be less reluctant to hire people because they feel that their employees—I mean, assuming that employers are reasonably kind-hearted and do not wish to make things difficult for their employees. Would it not therefore be easier for them to make the adjustment? That means that probably you would have fewer bankruptcies in the process of the adjustment.

LAIDLER—That really is the same point you made before. Firms would be more willing to fire people, people would be less worried about taking someone on out of sympathy—so the natural rate of unemployment would go up. I repeat, you get the inflation rate down through the unemployment mechanism by making people feel uncomfortable being unemployed. The more comfortable you make them feel, the longer you drag it out. I think we could erect arguments that would say that from a social point of view you are not doing anybody a favour by doing that. It is the same kind of argument that says it is nice for the person in the development area to be subsidised in order to stay in a job in a development area. But it is miserable for his children because they get born there and have to be subsidised in work there or are forced to move.

QUESTIONER—As a layman I understand the consequences you have described of the other school of thought, which leads in a measurable period of time to hyper-inflation, with all the consequences that might bring, not only economically but socially as well. What I did not understand was what are the consequences of the monetarist policy? If, for example, as you say, you cannot describe exactly how many unemployed there would be, but if 2 or 3 million people became unemployed as a result of this policy, however short-term, does this not create the same social problems that might arise from the mock-Keynesian philosophy with the same possible social disruption? In other words, does it achieve anything for the country as a whole?

LAIDLER—The country is in a miserable situation and you are not going to get out of it without further misery. And that is the first fact which must be faced—there is no painless cure. What is now being called the gradualist monetarist position I take to be simply the good economist's prescription. It is gradual precisely because we know enough now about the processes to be able to say the longer you take about the adjustment, the less will be the level of unemployment while it is going on. I don't think we know enough to be able to quantify that precisely. And in particular I certainly am now on the record—and if you like out on a limb—as having said that I think the contraction we now have is far too severe, and far too rapid. It is outrageous that politicians of all parties (and the press) should be saying: we must not have unemployment as a cure for inflation—we will not tolerate that—when 12 months ago they set in motion the policies to cause unemployment. And those policies are likely to do exactly that on a scale that no monetarist has ever prescribed.

QUESTIONER—Could I ask a sort of expository question which arises very much from the last one. It seems that 90 per cent of the people in this room agree with Professor Laidler, and I dare say we are going to discover in half an hour's time that 80 per cent agree with Professor Friedman—I think he's too controversial a pundit to expect a higher figure than that. But how about the others who, however unjustifiably, call themselves Keynesians, and pursue these policies of bad economics. Are we to assume that they are just bad economists? or that they pursue bad economic policy because what they recommend is vitiated by what they conceive, or have been told, is politically possible?

LAIDLER—The quick answer is that when political and economic reality meet it is economic reality that wins. An economist does no service by bending to what he is told is a matter of political reality, if he thinks that the economic reality is not consistent with it. But the economics, I really must emphasise, is bad economics. I do not know whether they have read the literature; certainly they have not provided in the scholarly journals the evidence which you would have expected them to provide if their position was to be taken seriously. I know it is difficult for a lay audience to believe that this is the case, but it *is* the case.

SAMUEL BRITTAN—I just want as an economic journalist—to be defined as a casual empiricist—to give a quick answer to that question about whether people in Whitehall and the National Institute are idiots or whether they are amateur politicians. Some of them, I'm sure, have read the literature, all the papers you are referring to. The trouble is that people who formulate the structure of the models on which decisions are taken try to incorporate what they call 'political realism' into their economic models. As I think Milton Friedman pointed out in a book published in the early 1950s, economists are very bad at predicting what is and what is not politically possible. The result is a bastard sort of model, which is bad economic theory and bad political theory. But that is the kind of model on which they operate. If it were as simple as there being not enough young men in the Treasury economic section who read certain articles, our problems would be very easy. But it is endemic in the whole way in which political decisions are taken in this country and the way in which our whole administrative structure operates.

5. Inflation, Taxation, Indexation

MILTON FRIEDMAN

*Professor of Economics,
University of Chicago*

THE AUTHOR

MILTON FRIEDMAN was born in 1912 in New York City and graduated from Rutgers before taking his MA at Chicago and PhD at Columbia. From 1935-37 he worked for the US National Resources Committee and from 1941-43 for the US Treasury.

Since 1946 he has taught at the University of Chicago, where he is the Paul Snowden Russell Distinguished Service Professor of Economics. He has taught also at the universities of Minnesota, Wisconsin, Columbia and California, as well as lecturing at universities throughout the world from Cambridge to Tokyo.

He is known to a wider audience as an advocate of a volunteer army (in place of the US draft), reverse income tax (in place of partial or universalist poverty programmes), monetary policy and floating exchange rates. He is the acknowledged head of the 'Chicago School' which specialises in the empirical testing of policy propositions derived from market analysis.

Among his best known books are *Essays in Positive Economics* (Chicago, 1953), *Studies in the Quantity Theory of Money* (edited by Friedman, Chicago, 1956), *A Theory of the Consumption Function* (Princeton, 1957), *Capitalism and Freedom* (Chicago, 1962), (with Anna J. Schwartz) *A Monetary History of the United States, 1867-1960* (Princeton, 1963), and *The Optimum Quantity of Money* (Aldine, Chicago, and Macmillan, London, 1969). His *Monetary Correction* was published by the IEA as Occasional Paper 41 in July 1974.

We are economists. We believe that the market operates, and that the market operates no less in the political sphere than it does in the economic sphere. We have bad economic policies because that is what the market wants to buy; that is where the profit is. We have bad economic advice provided to our political authorities because that is where the market is, because there is a demand for such advice and some people will arise to meet that demand.

Our big problem in getting the right ideas across is in part a marketing problem. We have to create a demand for those right ideas. On the subject of indexing, I think it is important to distinguish between indexing which should be legislated and compulsory and indexing which should be encouraged and voluntary. I believe that taxation should be compulsorily indexed in order to improve the political institutions under which we operate.

Taxation without representation

In a way the argument for indexing both taxes and government borrowing has only an incidental relation to the present problem of inflation. Its fundamental purpose, in my opinion, is to improve our political institutions. As I have repeatedly said, inflation is a form of taxation without representation. It is the kind of tax that can be imposed without being legislated by the authorities and without having to employ additional tax collectors. In making that statement for this more sophisticated audience I have to distinguish various components of inflation. The direct inflation tax is a tax on cash balances. If prices rise by 10 per cent per year, people have to collect more of these pieces of paper that are labelled pounds in order to keep the purchasing power of their cash balances constant. And those extra pieces of paper are the equivalent of vouchers certifying to the payment of a tax.

That part of the tax imposed by inflation will not be affected one way or the other by indexing. But there are two other components of the inflation tax. One component is that if personal and corporate income taxes are levied in nominal terms, in terms of pounds or dollars, inflation makes the effective rate of tax higher than it otherwise would be. I don't know what the numerical values are here, but roughly in the United States if personal incomes rise by 10 per cent because of an inflationary rise in prices of 10 per cent, so that in real terms incomes stay the same, personal taxes on the average go up by 15 per cent. That is because people are shoved up into higher tax brackets. In the same way, the corporate, or what you call company, taxation is very much increased by inflation because depreciation allowances, deductions for inventory, tend to be based on original costs rather than on market value. As a result much of what is reported as business profits is a purely paper profit and not a real profit, and the effect of imposing taxes on those paper profits is to impose a wealth tax on capital rather than an effective tax on the returns from capital.

I have made some calculations for the United States of that magnitude. For the United States that effect alone seems to have amounted to something like 15 billion dollars in the past year. The return from that hidden tax was twice as large as the direct return from the straight tax on cash balances—from the printing of paper money *per se*. I am going to speak much more from the experience in my own country than yours. I have talked with numbers of Senators and Representatives, and everyone of them says the same thing: they never would have legislated the present level of taxes deliberately and explicitly. They are appalled at what has happened to the real level of taxes. And yet they have of course benefitted from it and permitted it to occur in an indirect way through inflation. So I think the indexation of governmental taxes is essential to improve the political structure, to make legislators face up to their responsibilities for the taxes they impose as well as for the expenditures they legislate.

The technicalities of indexing

In technical detail what is required here is very straightforward and simple in the main. There are some complicated elements to it; I do not want to make it over-simple, but I know in our country, and I am sure this carries over to your country, the essential requirements are, first, that the personal exemptions be expressed in pounds multiplied by a price index. We have a low income allowance—you probably have some similar kind of an allowance—and an automatic deduction or something; whatever it is, it should likewise be expressed in pounds multiplied by an index number. The tax brackets should be expressed not as zero to £1,000, or whatever your surtax brackets are, but as zero to £1,000 multiplied by the price index, so that every year they would be adjusted automatically for inflation. The base for calculating capital gains should be adjusted for the change in price between time of purchase and time of sale. The base for calculating depreciation should be similarly adjusted; so should the base for calculating inventory costs. In principle, you ought to include in profit the gain through the reduction in the real value of obligations expressed in fixed nominal amounts. That ought to be included. There are also some other complications, but the things I have described would eliminate the bulk of the effects of inflation on the real tax rate.

On the side of government borrowing I likewise feel that this is a case of morality and fairness as much as it is of easing the transition. As I have stated several times here, I was myself converted to the issue of government purchasing power securities on a day in 1942 or 1943 when as a very young civil servant in the US Treasury Department I was asked to write a speech for the then Secretary Morganthau to exhort the public to buy US savings bonds. I found it impossible to write an honest speech.

I believe it is absolutely disgraceful that a democracy should demand of its high public officials that they lie to the people they are talking to, and knowingly lie. It is on that ground more than any other that I have ever since that day in 1942 or 1943 been in favour of purchasing power securities being issued by the government.

The argument made against this is the argument Mr Pepper raised again today. It is the argument which the US Treasury Department offered in 1952, when the Joint Economic Committee, as part of a series of hearings on monetary and debt problems, asked academic economists what they thought of purchasing power securities. A very large fraction of academic economists were then in favour of them. The Treasury gave its standard answer, which is exactly the answer in effect that Mr Pepper is giving today, if I understood him, which was that it would be undesirable to issue purchasing power securities because that would remove an anti-inflationary element from the economy because, they said, if we index—if we have purchasing power securities—inflation will add to our expenditure, whereas at present our expenditures stay the same in nominal dollars, our income is raised, and therefore we have an automatic anti-inflationary force.

The Keynesian theory

That argument is capable of being logically valid but I think it is not empirically relevant. It implicitly assumes that somehow or other the total expenditures of governments are independent of their sources of revenue. A great fallacy in much of the so-called Keynesian analysis has been to suppose that you can treat expenditures as if they were determined by one set of considerations and taxes as if they were determined by another. It is also the great fallacy of people who believe themselves to be in favour of fiscal responsibility—in the United States of many of the Republicans who have preached fiscal responsibility for many years. You have had the peculiar result in the United States over and over again that the Democrats have legislated the expenditures and the Republicans have legislated the taxes to pay for them—under the guise of fiscal responsibility.

Experience by this time has demonstrated Parkinson's law beyond the shadow of a doubt: that legislators will spend whatever the tax system will raise plus a good deal more. And therefore the only effective way to impose fiscal discipline is to reduce tax revenues. Therefore I myself have been converted to the policy of being in favour of tax reductions under any circumstances, for any excuse, for any reason, at any time.

To go back to purchasing power securities, if the government is going to be responsible and stop inflation, it costs nothing to issue a purchasing power security. Indeed the government will gain because they can sell those securities at better terms than they can sell the others. On the other hand, if the government is not going to be responsible, then it does seem to be extremely undesirable, immoral or whatever other word you want to use, for the government to argue that we cannot issue purchasing power securities because we need this check to keep us responsible. If they are going to be responsible they do not need to worry about any costs imposed by purchasing power securities. And if they are going to be irresponsible, purchasing power securities are needed all the more in order to protect the innocent public from the legislators whom they elected—erroneously.

I'm not sure I have completely answered Mr Pepper's point in that comment and I hope he will come back and pin me down on any further issues in that respect: I interpreted his question to be that if governments are not responsible, will purchasing power bonds make the inflation all the worse because it will increase governmental expenditure? The answer, to repeat it, is: the additional expenditures it will increase are far less harmful to the body politic than the alternative expenditures they will replace.

Voluntary indexation

For the rest, I am not in favour of legislating indexing. I am in favour of encouraging the voluntary adoption of indexing on as wide a scale as possible. And in this position I am in a long and distinguished line. Running back to well before Alfred Marshall, the first evidence of indexing is in Britain in the 14th century when your legislature required the colleges of Oxford and Cambridge to get at least one-third of their rent on their lands in corn, which one-third three centuries later was essentially 100 per cent of their rent. Marshall favoured it, William Stanley Jevons favoured it, Irving Fisher favoured it, John Maynard Keynes favoured it—surprisingly enough.[1] So that I am not here expressing anything of a special view. One of the interesting features I want to call to your attention is that many of the earlier arguments for indexing were as a means of mitigating the undesirable effects of *falling* prices. Marshall, when he wrote in 1885, was writing in a period when you were experiencing a price fall, and in the 1830s or 1820s some of the people who were then advocating indexing were doing so as a way of mitigating the harm being done by the post-Napoleonic war deflation. So that it is not true, as people often say, that those who are proposing indexing are simply proposing that we live with inflation. That is true in a way, but indexing is also a good vehicle for living with deflation.

However, a good money, a responsible money, is a better vehicle than indexing. Indexing is not in and of itself a desirable thing. It is —as I've sometimes said—a second-best device for a first-best world; but it is a first-best device for a second-best world. And the world is unfortunately second-best. At the same time, I see no reason why you should require by law that everybody index—this is what Brazil does—and in their circumstances it has been very effective and the results have been very good. However, I think they have gone much farther than would be desirable for us to go. What we ought to do is to encourage private indexing but not require it.

---

[1] Cf. Brian Griffiths, 'English Classical Political Economy and the Debate on Indexation', in *Monetary Correction*, Occasional Paper 41, IEA, 1974.

How do we encourage it? In the first place, the tax changes I have suggested would go a long way to encourage it. If the government offered a purchasing power security, the competition in the private financial market would force private enterprise to issue purchasing power securities as well. Even if the government does not issue a purchasing power security, private enterprises of course are going to offer purchasing power securities. The trend has already started: it is very well advanced in the United States. Empirically speaking, the short-term interest rate has been roughly equal to the rate of rise in prices over the prior several years plus about 3 per cent. And hence the whole series of floating notes, like the Citicorp floating notes in which the rate of return promised is a certain number of points above the Treasury bill rate or a short-term market rate, is economically equivalent to a purchasing power security. That kind of variable interest rate note has already started to spread very widely both in the United States and elsewhere, so you are getting a lot of indexing of that kind.

Escalator clauses

In the wage field in the United States there are something like 10 million union employees covered by cost-of-living escalator clauses. In Britain you did an unwise thing in imposing by legislation a threshold agreement: that was undesirable because it was exactly this imposition of a *general* rule rather than allowing the arrangements to be reached in the *individual* case. But I think that you would and should have a large number of voluntary wage agreements which include an escalator clause.

In many areas now of course there are escalator clauses. You have rental leases which are a fraction of gross; you have automobile insurance policies which pay costs of repairing; all of these have implicit escalator clauses in them. And you are going to have a much wider extension of that kind of escalator clause. The government could encourage it, as I say, first, by setting an example by establishing a kind of instrument through its purchasing power security, second, by the tax changes I have described. Because, under present circumstances, if an enterprise were to offer a purchasing power security, the adjustment for inflation would be subject to income tax as well as the real interest rate paid. The changes I have suggested in the personal and company tax would in effect eliminate that, because you would adjust the capital gains basis, and therefore the adjustment for inflation would not be subject to income tax. I think those are the most effective ways in which the government could encourage it.

Now I do not know about your case. In the United States there is one other major area, where I think the government will have to encourage it. This is the so-called thrift institutions.

The financial intermediaries

We have in the United States, as you have here, savings and loan associations,[2] mutual savings banks, and so on, of very major magnitude. Their total liabilities at the moment are something like $400 billion. These institutions have been 'gambling' for quite a long time by lending long and borrowing short and they are now stuck with a portfolio of lower interest rates than those they now have to pay if they are to keep the funds on deposit with them. If you were to do a proper accounting analysis, there is hardly one of them today that is not *technically* 'bankrupt' in the sense that the market value of its assets is less than the market value of its liabilities.

Being a hard-boiled believer in a free market, I might like to see the market solution work itself out and let a lot of them go broke. But I rather doubt whether that will happen. I rather suspect they will be bailed out by government. I hate like the devil to enter into political prophecy, but this is one of the easiest of any you might make because it has already occurred. There have already been a series of measures to bail them out. But they have been of the wrong kind consistent with the government trying to prop up the value of their capital assets. Along that line you are in a bottomless pit. If you really try to save the savings and loan associations by propping up the market value of their assets, you are going to have to create a quantity of money in the process that is going to blow the lid off the inflation. What is the alternative?

The least bad alternative would be for the government to subsidise thrift institutions on the income side, but subject to the proviso that as a condition of assisting them they must move entirely to an index

---

[2] [The British equivalent is the building societies. The fundamental difference is that the US institutions lend with fixed interest rates, whereas building society mortgages have variable interest rates. Building societies also issue variable rate investments.—ED.]

basis for their assets and liabilities. They must convert to a variable interest rate mortgage which has the effect of being indexed. How you do it is important because some of the ways would not be very effective. You have to do it in a way in which the face value of the mortgage and not merely the repayments are indexed. You have to have a variable interest rate mortgage and you must offer your customers a variable interest deposit. If that were done, the subsidisation programme would automatically end because, as the portfolio turned over and became more and more indexed, you would eliminate the problem that started the process.

Beyond that I would leave it to the voluntary interests of people to engage in indexing and not try to enforce it in any way. The question comes up: what good does it do to have all these things indexed? The major objection I have heard arises out of a misconception. The objection I have heard here today and in Britain several times in the past few days is that somehow or other indexing would prevent real wages from being reduced where it is economically necessary for them to be reduced. Indexing prevents no such thing. Indexing is a provision to adjust contractual terms between re-contracting. When a new contract is negotiated, it can be at a higher or a lower or any real wage whatsoever. All that indexing does is to say: whatever two people agree on, they will in fact achieve. It is only a way of enabling people to engage in effective contracts. Today, if a contract is made between an employer and, let us say, a trade union or a non-union group, both of them have to make a guess about the rate of inflation. If they agree on the rate of inflation, they will build party has engaged in a contract he did not voluntarily engage in: it into their contracted increase.

If the actual rate of inflation is equal to the anticipated rate, nobody is disappointed and there is no distortion. But if the actual rate of inflation is different from the expected rate, one or the other party has engaged in a contract he did not voluntarily engage in: he's got distorted terms. It is this feature that is largely responsible for the unemployment which results from a slowing down of the rate of inflation that is *not* anticipated and that has not been built into these contracts. By indexing you eliminate that disappointment and distortion. Parties can contract to whatever terms they want. They can contract in real terms.

I said earlier that I thought it cleared the mind analytically to try to carry out an analysis in a world of complete indexing. But it not only clears the mind; it also in practice would prevent some of the adverse effects from slowing down inflation, or some of the adverse effects from an acceleration of inflation. It is on those grounds that I think indexing would be extremely useful and I think it is in that area that the experience of Brazil is most important.

Indexing and authoritarianism

I hesitate to refer to Brazil because I have been burned so badly. The moment I refer to Brazil I am told: Oh, you like a military dictatorship? No, I do not: military dictatorships are terrible. But I think as scientists we ought to pick up our data wherever we can get them, from communist Russia, from Nazi Germany, from totalitarian Brazil, from wherever we can get good economic evidence. We do not have enough data so that we can afford to let our scientific analyses be determined by our political sympathies.

And the evidence from Brazil and from other countries is very striking. It is that you can greatly reduce distortion by a widespread use of indexing.

DISCUSSION

GEORGE SCHWARTZ—With the 'greenback' debacle in the middle of the 19th century private people did index their contracts by inserting a gold clause. What happened to that solemn contract between private people agreeing that the terms of the contract should be based on the gold clause? It was arbitrarily abrogated by the Roosevelt administration. Are you in the US going to write a guarantee into your constitution?—We can't because we haven't got a constitution! What guarantee is there with any of these methods? In my lifetime government has proved to be a liar, a thief and a cheat. And I don't see any difference today.

FRIEDMAN—I have no answer to the fundamental question of guarantees but I do think it is important to understand the gold clause a little better. It is rather more complicated than George Schwartz's intervention might suggest.

I agree with him that the Supreme Court should not have abrogated it. But it is interesting to read the relevant decisions of the Supreme Court. In large part they rested on the fact that while the gold clause was entered into to protect people in real value, enforcement of the gold clause would not achieve that purpose. The argument which induced a majority of the Supreme Court justices to abrogate the gold clause was that in 1933, when the issue arose, although the gold price had risen in nominal terms, the level of prices of goods and services in general had fallen, and so the majority on the Supreme Court said that people who were being paid back in dollars were already making one gain from the decline of the price level. It was not in the interests of equity and justice that they should make a second gain because the dollar price of gold was being raised by the authorities.

It turns out on reading those decisions that had those clauses been purchasing power clauses it is very far from clear that the US Supreme Court would have abrogated them. This is a footnote to history and does not alter your main point that I have no more assurance that a privately arranged escalator contract will be enforced in the Courts than I have that any other private contract will be enforced in the Courts. I don't see anything special about it. On your grounds you would suppose that nobody would enter into any contract because there is no contract that you can be sure will be enforced.

NICHOLAS RIDLEY[1]—I would like to go back to the question of the indexed government securities Professor Friedman talked about. When I approached British Treasury Ministers asking why they did not introduce an indexed government security, they said that it would do too much harm to the values of the existing government debt. We have a nominal of about £30,000 million worth of government debt, which is currently valued in the markets at about £14,000 million, having gone down £5,000 million in the last year. If it dropped another £10,000 million due to the issue of an indexed bond this would obviously be very serious politically to the poor mugs who still hold war loan. Would Professor Friedman comment on that argument? Would the higher interest rate check too much selling and bring in buyers as it started to rise? Does he believe there would be serious disruptive effects upon existing holders of government stock if fully indexed bonds were issued?

FRIEDMAN—That is a very good, a very fundamental, question. Let us take it up a little bit at a time, because it is necessary to proceed piecemeal.

---

[1] Parliamentary Under-Secretary of State, Department of Trade and Industry, 1970-72.

82

The question is at what rate the indexed bonds are going to be issued. One way would be to auction them off. That might lead to a negative real rate being set by the market. If you conceive of governments issuing their indexed bonds by auctioning them off, but with the index clause inserted, there is no reason why that should produce any serious disruption whatsoever to the value of outstanding securities. Gradually as time went on, as more and more indexed bonds were sold in the market, the real rate offered would have to go up. But if without indexing inflation accelerates, the value of these bonds is going to fall anyway. If inflation decelerates, it will go the opposite way. If indeed the issuance of indexed bonds is accompanied by a responsible monetary policy which produces a deceleration of inflation, you will suffer no loss in the market value of the other bonds. On the contrary, they will rise. If it is accompanied by an irresponsible policy, you will indeed suffer a loss on the other bonds, as you would anyway. So I really do not think that, once you look at it in that realistic way of issuing these bonds on an auction basis, you will necessarily get into any kind of problem at all.

LORD ROBBINS—You have to remember that opinion in Whitehall to some extent is governed, although perhaps now unconsciously, by a dictum of the late Arthur Balfour who was one of the few intellectuals who have been Prime Minister of this country: he said that no government is prepared to legislate on the assumption of its own irresponsibility.

FRIEDMAN—I agree, and I do not want them to do that. I want them to legislate on the assumption of their *responsibility*, because that means it costs them nothing if they are really responsible. It not only costs them nothing to issue indexed bonds—they gain, because they can issue them at a *negative* interest rate to begin with.

GORDON PEPPER—Having been invited to make a rejoinder—I have no argument at all about the morals. I am assuming that we have a government that does immoral things, and which is capable of expanding the money supply in the same way as in 1972-73. If I heard correctly, you argued that index-linking helps even if inflation is accelerating. I did not fully follow and I do not fully understand.

I am afraid that what happened after the introduction of floating exchange rates may happen with index-linking. After floating exchange rates were introduced, the government followed a completely irresponsible monetary policy—the resulting downward movement in sterling accelerated inflation. We have only a limited period of time before the height of inflation in this country undermines our democratic structure. During that period we must try to educate MP's, people in Whitehall and people in power. I do not want to see the government misusing index-linking—making mistakes similar to 1972-73 and causing inflation to accelerate that much faster. We may have only one more cycle rather than another two or three cycles.

The other point which I tried to make earlier concerns indexing of wages. If, because of practical reasons of one form or another, it is impossible to index wages, is not some form of wages policy a second best method of trying to bias the outcome of a reduction in the rate of growth of the money supply towards a greater reduction in price inflation and a smaller reduction in real economic activity?

FRIEDMAN—Those are very good questions. With respect, I would like to enter a demur about the floating exchange rate aspect. I think it was irresponsible government policy that made it necessary to devalue. It was a continuation of irresponsible government policy that caused further depreciation. I think it is irresponsible government policy today in your country that is keeping the exchange rate up. From the long-run point of view—if I understand your situation properly—it just seems to me insane for your government to be giving exchange guarantees on any large amount of sterling whether to oil countries or anybody else. As I understand it, they have been doing that. Is that right? So I do not believe you can blame the floating exchange rates for the irresponsible policies, but quite the other way around.

On your direct question: let us answer the question, how is it that index-linking of bonds would accelerate inflation? Mr Pepper would undoubtedly reply that, if you index-link the bonds, then as time passes, as inflation accelerates, your necessary governmental expenditures are increased. That is true. The question is *how* you index-link bonds. You can index-link bonds in two very different ways. One way is by saying that the maturity value or face value will at the time of redemption be multiplied by an index number, and the annual coupon will be multiplied by an index number, so that a bond that would otherwise pay a £3 per £100 yield would pay £3·30 if inflation were 10 per cent. But the face value instead of being £100 would now be raised to £110.

The other way is to pay each year the face coupon rate plus the rate of inflation. So the face value would remain £100, and you would pay £3 plus £10, that is 13 per cent. Now it may look as if this second way gets you into the dilemma you're speaking of, whereas the first does not. But that is wrong, they are both equivalent. The second way essentially involves your paying off the debt, you are amortising the debt, that 10 per cent payment means that you are reducing the real burden of the debt and therefore you can afford to borrow more, as it were, at the same interest rate. So that the effect of indexing is not to add to your annual interest payment requirements the rate of inflation times the debt, but only the rate of inflation times the interest payments. In terms of magnitude I am suggesting to you that what you are talking about is much smaller than you might otherwise suppose.

Now offsetting this effect, which no doubt is there in that indexing would tend to increase expenditure on interest payments, is that it would tend to reduce other expenditures. If we go back to the principle I was citing earlier, which I think is true: that what is really given to you more or less is the deficit which a government is willing to run, so that total expenditures are determined by adding to that deficit whatever the tax system will yield—the major effect in my opinion of indexing would be that the heavier pressure of interest payments to meet the indexed security rates would impose on you the necessity of cutting other expenditure.

Finally, suppose you do not index. Then you have a situation in which it is extremely hard to sell long-dated securities. I am sure that as a stockbroker you do not have as good a market for long-dated securities now as you had in the period when prices were stable. But if you sell short-dated securities, the market imposes the effect of indexing on the Treasury because you can sell short-dated securities only at a price which allows for the anticipated inflation. For a long time you have been able to con the purchasers into believing that the rate of inflation was going to be less than it was. But doesn't that come to an end? And may it not indeed be that the effect of not indexing will be to make the annual expenditures of the government on interest higher than with indexed bonds, because expectations will run ahead of the reality and force up the interest rates the government has to pay, even higher than would be enough to justify it. All I am trying to argue is that there are forces running in different directions.

Incomes 'policies': the case of Argentina

Now let me go to your other question about wages policy. I want to associate myself with one of the comments of David Laidler. (I hope it's safe to say at this time and in this place and in this country that he got some of his training at the University of Chicago.) I want to associate myself very much with his comment about not using the phrase 'wage policies or incomes policies' if what you mean is governmental *control* of wages and prices. We in the United States have got very badly hurt by that misuse of terminology. And you also are likely to. People say to me that by 'incomes policy' all they mean is improving the markets and letting the free markets operate. I am for those kinds of incomes policies. But what you are really talking about is whether the fixing of wages and prices could enable you to achieve an easier transition. I cannot rule out the possibility completely, because I know of one empirical case in which it did work—the case of Argentina. One year back in the 1960s a government was determined to end an inflation—a rare event in Argentina! It was very substantial, not your moderate kind of inflation. It was about 40-50 per cent. They announced a new monetary policy which was going to be very strict and they accompanied it by a temporary fixing of prices and wages. By altering people's expectations, and cutting off the tendency for wages to rise in line with anticipated inflation, they did succeed in rather substantially reducing the rate of inflation with relatively little cost in the way of unemployment. Needless to say, this was a temporary success. It was followed by another blow-up a few years later. So it is hardly a permanent answer.

I cannot rule out the theoretical possibility that a measure like that might be to some extent successful. But that is a very exceptional case. It was possible only because you were dealing with rates of inflation of 40 or 50 per cent. When you deal with what are really relatively low rates of inflation you are not proposing this wage and price freeze or control for more than six months. Let us leave out all political considerations for a moment; let us suppose you can do it for a six-month period. Then what are you doing?

Let us suppose you are faced with a 20 per cent inflation. You are trying to change people's expectations from a 10 per cent rise in prices over that period to, say, a zero per cent rise in prices. In the process you are preventing changes in *relative* prices and wages, many of which will be multiples of 10 per cent. So you are introducing a whole series of *distortions* of a very considerable kind into your price structure. You can have exactly the same result far better if, without any wage policy, the people can be made to believe that the government is serious in its anti-inflation effort. In reality your wage proposal will not work unless people believe the government is serious.

The next stage of getting away from this purely hypothetical case of the best of all circumstances is the reality that wage and price controls will be adopted only as a means of enabling the government to inflate more than it otherwise would. Those of you who argue for wage and price policy on this kind of a valid argument are in fact lending support to an inflationary policy, because the empirical evidence is that every government imposes wage and price controls when it intends to inflate.

It does so because it wants to give the public the impression that it is doing something about inflation when it really does not want to do something. That describes Mr Heath's freeze here. It describes Mr Nixon's freeze in August 1971. Let me supplement David Laidler's historical account of the British experience with an account of the American experience, which is equally informative.

American experience

In 1969-70 we adopted a restraining monetary policy. It worked like a charm. The rate of price inflation fell from roughly 7 per cent sometime in 1969 to something like $4\frac{1}{2}$ per cent at the time of the freeze on 15 August, 1971. So in about 15 or 16 months we had come down from something like 7 per cent (which had been accelerating, so that the real comparison is between where it *would* have gone to with *continuation* of prior inflation) to 4 per cent with the mildest recession in the post-war period.

In 1970-71 the economy had already turned up: we were expanding. The rate of inflation was still coming down. But two events occurred. One was that the consequences of our mistaken gold policy were finally coming home to roost, and something had to be done to close the gold window. The other was that there was still a lagged reaction to earlier experience which was leading politicians of all parties to yell and scream about how terrible the recession was: we were not moving fast enough and had to move faster. All of this was combined with Mr Nixon's great concern for a favourable economic climate for the 1972 election. The combination of these events led him on 15 August, 1971 to close the gold window—which by itself would have been very unpopular—and to cover it up with the price and wage freeze and with an announcement of measures intended to stimulate employment. There is no doubt that the price and wage freeze was undertaken in order to permit an inflationary policy to follow thereafter.

I believe our present situation dates precisely from that date; the origin of our troubles is there. As David Laidler said, the initial effects of an inflationary policy were on output, its subsequent effects on prices, though they were hidden for a time by the price and wage controls. The controls finally blew up and had to be abandoned. Our present recorded 12 per cent rate of inflation is a statistical fake. The true rate of inflation is not 12 per cent. Part of it is the unveiling of price increases that were suppressed during the price control period, and part of it is that every businessman who has any sense, which includes every businessman, is trying to get his base prices up as high as he can in case there is another price and wage freeze. And that is why the actual experience in the United States is that we are going to see a very sharp tapering off in the recorded rates of inflation.

This process is going to come to an end, the truth is going to be told, and you are going to have a recorded decline in the rate of inflation. The danger there is the one David Laidler mentioned, that everyone will breathe a sigh of relief and say—My God, isn't this wonderful! We're back at only 8 per cent inflation!—Only 8 per cent! —when it was $4\frac{1}{2}$ per cent when Nixon imposed price and wage control. And they are going to say: we have got to do something about unemployment . . .

LORD ROBBINS—Now it's 4 o'clock. We must not tax Professor Friedman too far.

FRIEDMAN—At least you ought to escalate the tax!

LORD ROBBINS—And we still have to hear a summing-up from a broad philosophical point of view from Mr Brittan.

6. Inflation and Government

SAMUEL BRITTAN

Principal economic commentator, 'Financial Times';
Visiting Fellow, Nuffield College, Oxford

THE AUTHOR

SAMUEL BRITTAN was born in 1933 and éducated at Kilburn Grammar School and Jesus College, Cambridge, where he took first-class honours in economics. He then held various posts on the *Financial Times* (1955-61); was Economics Editor of the *Observer* (1961-64); an Adviser at the Department of Economic Affairs (1965); and has been principal economic commentator on the *Financial Times* since 1966.

He was the first winner of the Senior Wincott Award for financial journalists in 1971. He was a Research Fellow of Nuffield College in 1973-4 and in 1974 was elected a Visiting Fellow of that College.

His publications include *Steering the Economy* (third edition, Penguin, 1971), *Left or Right: The Bogus Dilemma* (Secker & Warburg, 1968), *The Price of Economic Freedom: A Guide to Flexible Rates* (Macmillan, 1970), *Is There An Economic Consensus?* (Macmillan, 1973), and *Capitalism and the Permissive Society* (Macmillan, 1973).

I begin with a *mea culpa*. We must all learn from our mistakes. I supported the 1972 wage-price freeze—though not the subsequent phases 2 and 3—very much on the lines of the arguments from the Argentine case presented by Professor Milton Friedman. I thought it would be helpful in puncturing inflationary expectations in conjunction with—not a deflation, you must not use that word—but an anti-inflationary monetary and fiscal policy. Of course I should have realised more, after all these years, about the characters of the people enforcing it. It was in fact used, not as an accompaniment to sound monetary and fiscal policy, but as an excuse for pumping more money into the economy in the pursuit of so-called full employment. The result will probably be to land us eventually with the highest post-war rate of unemployment we have ever seen.

But I now move on to what Milton Friedman calls the marketing problem, because this is very important to me.

Imperfections of the political market

If it were not so late on in his visit, I would be very interested to hear his ideas for improving the political market. People talk a great deal about the imperfections of the commercial market, but the most imperfect market we have is the political market. This is the real problem, even more than inflation, that threatens western democracy at the moment.

I think that people who are called monetarists sometimes give an unnecessarily arid and misleading impression of their own case by the way in which it is often presented in popular discussion. They give the impression that it is something rather technical to do with the money supply; and the Bank of England should be left to get on with it. It is made to seem like a very technical argument about M1 and M3 and disintermediation. First of all, the most important proposition relates to money *expenditure*. The view that the most important influence on money expenditure is the money supply is, I think, valid; but most of what we are saying would be equally true if it turned out empirically that budgetary policy was more important.

Second, there is something even more important than that. (This is why I think the label 'monetarist' is so awful and the label 'neo-classical' is even more awful, but I wish I could think of a better one.) The central point that sound economists are making is that there is no easy way by which the government can create a lower rate of unemployment than is allowed by the workings of the economy with all its imperfections, by the state of the labour market, and by all the other real forces at work. We are too much influenced by the situation in the 1930s when what was required was an increase in the money supply instead of a reduction in the level of money wages. This is not the situation now.

'Mass unemployment' scare

The central point of the position—and I am putting this across really for the benefit of the sceptics in this room who have not been as vocal as they should be—the central point of what is miscalled the monetarist position, is that we cannot spend our way into as low a rate of unemployment as we would like. The so-called monetarists are not advocating mass unemployment. Their argument in the current UK context is that we are going to get the unemployment in any event. The question is whether we get it now at a still moderate rate of inflation or whether we get it later at a state of hyper-inflation, when possibly, owing to the breakdown of the monetary system, we will have a real depression and not a recession. What we are saying is that you do not avoid the unemployment that you are going to get by the normal U-turns and by printing money.

Most of us say, whenever we are confronted with people like Milton Friedman and David Laidler, that we agree with 90 per cent of what they say. I think I know them well enough to say that this is more irritating to them than to have out-and-out opponents. I remember my tutorials with Milton Friedman many years ago and I know how that remark irritates him. But most of us, being human, are in that position: people do not agree with each other 100 per cent. Now 5 per cent of my queries (rather than disagreements) are of a kind which can only be discussed in what would really have to be a tutorial. But the other 5 per cent relate to what could be termed the political marketing of what one might call the market economy case. Unfortunately there is mainly a market for this case only in the Conservative party, perhaps a tiny fraction of the Liberal party and an even tinier fraction of the Labour party. Anybody who knows my political record will know that it does not give me any pleasure to put it that way, but that is the position.

Funny alliance?

The impression gained is that there is a funny kind of alliance between the extreme left and the extreme right in saying that unions are wonderful. I think too that, in the heat of the moment, a good many Conservatives and others, in an understandable reaction to the policies of the last Conservative Government in the past couple of years, which attempted to substitute price and incomes control for a sensible economic policy, have made the mistake of almost whitewashing the unions. Anybody who has listened to Milton Friedman and read carefully what he has written, will realise that the unions do do a great deal of damage. They create unemployment; they deprive people, usually poor people, of job opportunities; they price the most handicapped and the most unfortunate people either out of the labour market or into worse employment than they could otherwise get. And as we are tending to move into a new medievalism, into a new world of so-called 'just' but really very unjust prices, it might be worth pointing out, in medieval terms, that the unions are not the Robin Hoods they are supposed to be on every television programme. They are the robber barons of the system. And this is true even if they have zero effect on the rate of inflation.

I would like to argue and develop this a bit more in later discussion, but perhaps the best way of stating the case is to say that, if one takes a dynamic model which I might try and develop, the effects of unions in the real world are probably to raise the natural rate of unemployment rather than immediately to raise the rate of inflation. Of course governments do not like the natural rate of unemployment and from that follows all the consequences we have been talking about.

I believe in a social market economy, primarily for ethical reasons and because of a belief in personal freedom rather than because of anything to do with maximisation of the GNP. It is unfortunate that, in the way the political debate has focussed in this country, the whole case for a social market economy, everything represented by those economists who are still prepared to believe that relative prices matter, has become over-simplified into the word 'monetarism'. I mix with people in the twilight world between politics and economics and they all say to me: 'I wish you people would not talk exclusively about the money supply.' I sometimes quote to them a remark of Milton Friedman's which in turn derives from John Stuart Mill: The more I learn about money the more I realise how little it matters. But perhaps to get to a world in which we can forget about the money supply and talk about the real problems of resource allocation and genuine ways of alleviating poverty, as distinct from phoney and deceptive methods, such as rent controls and housing subsidies, we may have to get the inflationary psychosis out of the system.

Indexation and a genuine floating rate

Indexation has come up in basically two contexts: one is as an adjunct to a policy of gradually decelerating the growth of the money supply, and as a way of alleviating the unemployment consequences of so doing. If I were more politically optimistic I might leave it there. But I would still be prepared to support indexation, not just as an adjunct to a cure, but also as a method for enabling some semblance of civilised life to continue during what could be generations of currency disorders.

There is an analogy here in the case for floating rates—only unfortunately nothing in the world seems to be able to induce the Bank of England to operate a genuine floating rate. By that I do not mean 'clean' floating, I do not mean no intervention; I mean simply allowing market forces to influence the rate. We have had all the guarantees Milton Friedman has been talking about, plus many more that are secret, plus a good deal of public sector borrowing with no forward risk on the part of the borrower because the risks have all been taken by the central government. This is not any kind of floating rate, not even a 'dirty' floating rate. But taking the general international scene, I am quite sure that the adjustments to the real changes—such as the sudden eruption of the oil cartel—would have been far more difficult if we were still in a world of fixed rates.

I now come to the main analytical question which I would like to ask our distinguished Chairman and our monetarists. My friend Peter Jay is in the habit—he is not exactly a colourless character—of saying that medium-term stabilisation policy would involve tolerating unemployment in the low millions. Now there are basically three unemployment rates we have to consider.

First, there is the wishful thinking unemployment rate, the unemployment rate which exists either in White Papers or in supposedly secret drawers in Treasury offices—the unemployment rate that politicians or officials think they could achieve. We can, I think, forget about that.

Second, there is the so-called 'natural' rate of unemployment. Perhaps we ought to call it the *equilibrium* or *sustainable* rate of unemployment, which without institutional reform a system can settle down to at a constant rate of price change.

Third, there is the long-term question we ought to be discussing: how we can bring that rate down.

Fourth, there is the rather horrible question of the transitional rate of unemployment. Assume you want to go down from an underlying rate of inflation of 20 per cent to one of 10 per cent over four years, leaving out ripples on the route. The question one is always being asked by so-called 'practical' people is: what will be the transitional unemployment? It is quite understandably very difficult to get an answer. But the question is this: if we were to attempt to mitigate the hardship involved, say, by focussing government expenditure on the depressed areas, on the areas particularly hard-hit, would this be helpful?

I read a column in *Newsweek* by Professor Friedman in which he was very sceptical of the idea of special help for special areas. But suppose one puts this in the context of a budgetary ceiling and a determination not to finance any budgetary deficit by creating money, which in practice means a very low budgetary deficit. The question is not what the total size of the budget should be, but whether it should be spent in areas, say, in the South-East where employment is over-full, or whether it should be spent in areas which have regional problems where industries have declined, and where, given the rigidities of the wage structure, people cannot find work. If you switch your expenditures, switch given totals of expenditure towards hard-hit areas or towards certain industries, might you not be able to get a lower rate of transitional unemployment for the same effect on inflation? These are quite genuine, not rhetorical, questions.

DISCUSSION

LAIDLER—Mr Brittan raised a question of how much unemployment to reduce the inflation rate how fast? We do not know very much about it but we do have one observation which is the 1971-72 period when the unemployment rate peaked out at that magic number one million. I have the consumer price index in front of me in percentage rate of change terms. From the first/second quarter 1971 the inflation rate in this country (retail prices) was 11·9 per cent. From the first/second quarter 1972 it was 4·6 per cent. So you can more than halve that kind of inflation rate in a year with a million unemployed. And that is a very rapid decrease in the rate of inflation. I do not know, however, how far we can extrapolate from that experience to the next.

FRIEDMAN—There are many other cases. This is an important subject for study—and I hope there are some potential PhD students here because I think we need half-a-dozen dissertations on various episodes which could give us a better handle on this number. Let me give you some of the examples.

George Schwartz referred to the 'greenback' period, 1865-1879, when the price level was cut in half, unemployment was trivial, the fastest rate of growth of any decade in American history. That is a favourable case, although at the time there was a lot of yelling. France, 1925: a very effective, rapid stabilisation in which the inflation rate was reduced sharply, very little unemployment. Britain in the 1920s: a bad case, needed a 10 per cent decline in prices—result, very high unemployment for a long period. You have dozens of cases in South America and lots of other episodes. In many of those I know, you have had a very substantial reduction in inflation at very low cost.

LORD ROBBINS—What was the strength of the trade union movement in the greenback period, in France in the period you mentioned, and in this country in the 1920s?

FRIEDMAN—In the US it was negligible. I don't know about France.

LORD ROBBINS—It was pretty weak.

FRIEDMAN—It may well have been. In Britain in the 1920s it was pretty strong. I am not quarrelling with the view that the existence of a trade union may make this problem more difficult than it otherwise would be. One of the things we would hope would come from a serious study of the kind I am describing is how important these various factors are. But I want to emphasise it is not only trade unions that matter. Let me give you the comparison between the US, 1873 to 1879 and 1929 to 1932. You had essentially the same decline in nominal income in the two periods. The first was accompanied by rapid economic growth, a sharp fall in prices, and very little fall in employment. The second was accompanied by a sharp decline in employment, and a much slower decline in prices. Much more unemployment. Yet trade unions were not very strong in the United States in 1929-32. So I think the phenomena at work involve more than trade unions.

JOHN FLEMMING—I can offer a policy possibly superior to some of the versions of monetarism but liable to attract a label which would certainly be worse. If the risks, in terms of unemployment, associated with the kind of monetary policy which some people are advocating are very great, in the sense that they would commit themselves to a tight monetary policy although not knowing whether the resultant unemployment in 12 months' time was going to be half a million or one and a half million, it might be very substantially preferable to have a policy which was designed to bring about a certain very modest rate of increase in unemployment itself. Such a policy might have considerable advantages, given the ignorance that we are in about the effects of certain policies, over the adoption of a monetary rule. But it seems to me quite clear that, however modest one were to make the planned increase, one would receive even more abuse for advocating such a policy than the abuse that is already poured on the heads of monetarists.

LORD ROBBINS—Now I think the time has come to ask such of the speakers as are present, except the chairman, to make further observations on what has been raised in the course of the discussion.

LAIDLER—I would like to make two or three points. First, about wage and price controls: the standard case for them in this country has been that they affect expectations. That really is a very spurious argument, because any economic policy that is believed in will affect expectations—there is nothing unique about wage and price controls. And I would have thought, honestly, in the present situation that if there was one economic policy that nobody is going to believe in, when it is enforced, it is another bout of wage and price controls.

Second, there is some very simple economics that tells you why wage and price controls do not work. The market price is a price agreed between a buyer and a seller. Effective price control fixes a price below market price. That means there are buyers who are willing to pay a higher price and sellers who are willing to accept a higher price. Therefore you have the open possibility and incentive to collusion on both sides of the bargain. What then happens is that the least law-abiding among us start engaging in that kind of collusion. And the more law-abiding among us unfortunately are put in the position of either having to go without or break the law. This was brought home to me very strongly during the Heath freeze by a neighbour who has a number of factories; he told me 'Quite frankly, next week either we start breaking the law like our competitors or we start closing down our factories'. And that is appalling—absolutely appalling. I think we should remember what wage and price controls do to business morality and respect for the law.

Third, the more technical business about what you might want to do in order to bring the rate of monetary expansion under control. We have a set of monetary institutions in this country that go under the title 'Competition and Credit Control'. Lately there has been quite a stirring in the press to the effect that Competition and Credit Control is a monetarist invention and the one place where the monetarists went wrong—Patrick Cosgrave said exactly that in the *Spectator* a few weeks ago.

The problem of Competition and Credit Control is that it does not have enough of either. It does not have enough competition because the building societies were explicitly given a privileged position. A great deal of the monetary expansion in the last few years in this country has come through attempts to use monetary policy to keep interest rates down and protect owner-occupiers. Now of course it has not protected owner-occupiers; it has put them much further out on a limb than they otherwise would have been; and they are all in a much worse position now than they would have been if this policy had never been followed in the first place. There are people now whose entire equity in their houses has been wiped out in the last 12 months, who are faced with cash flow problems with their mortgages, and who just cannot cope.

As for the credit control side of it, we have a system—heaven help us!—of reserve assets that includes short-term government securities. This means that having got a good short-term government securities market, which gave us the chance of insulating monetary policy from the government borrowing requirement, we have thrown away that advantage. The second thing we have is a system in which the banking system can actually manufacture its own reserve assets by lending at call to the discount market. I do not believe that it is possible to conduct the kind of monetary policy that I would advocate, and Milton Friedman would advocate, while we have that institutional set-up. I do not understand why we cannot have a simple rule that says: commercial banks must hold cash or deposits with the Bank of England at least equal to 10 per cent or 18 per cent or 15 per cent of their deposit liabilities, and leave it at that.

MILTON FRIEDMAN—There are a number of comments I would like to make. One goes back to Lionel Robbins's earlier discussion of three propositions. The first one was: do we agree that the control of the credit base is an indispensable condition of coping with inflation? We all said yes. The second one was: inflation is always caused by failure to observe prescription number one. I want to make a comment on that. I have for years been trying to collect examples or counter-examples to that proposition. I have almost never addressed a group of economists without asking them if any of them had one. And I have myself discovered one and only one counter-example. That is the Korean war inflation in the United States in 1950-51, which is the one case I know of a pretty substantial rate of price rise which cannot be attributed to a prior excessive expansion of the quantity of money, but rather was due to an autonomous explosion in the velocity of circulation. Now it is an interesting exception because, to put that old aphorism correctly, it's an exception that tests the rule. It was very brief because it was not supported by monetary expansion. And the rate of inflation in the United States came down from something like 15 or 20 per cent in wholesale prices to something like zero per cent within six months, because there was no support for this autonomous explosion in velocity.

I do not know of any other example. I think it would be interesting to collect all such other examples that anybody can find. I have brought this up in order to express my usual plea. If there is anybody who knows of any case that could with any plausible reason be regarded as an exception, I would appreciate very much if he would let me know.

LORD ROBBINS—This is a convenient moment to make this point. There are almost endless ambiguities in social and historical explanations aroused by the term 'cause'. I am not quite sure whether you were here when Professor Coats indulged in his very entertaining historical reflections. It seemed to me then that historians whose views he was drawing our attention to were people who were prepared to or anxious to take things further back as the sort of explanation which we as economists would think appropriate. And one can argue almost indefinitely about semantics. Bob Coats mentioned some historic cases of inflation, the silver inflation of the Renaissance and the German inflation, and so on, and the varying explanations given by historians. Clearly the historians were looking for something other than what economists would react to. He did not mention the episode of the Assignats which I think is extraordinarily interesting from our point of view. You had a revolution, you had people with new ideas of what government should do. They went all out for a kind of money which was bound to break down by indefinite multiplication. Now we, as economists, would say that a sufficient explanation is that they did issue the money. But supposing an historian should say: 'Oh, about the cause of that'—I am improvising entirely, I am not expert at all in the details of the history—'the cause was that some of the Jacobins can be shown to have had very unfortunate experiences with their parents, and consequently they took a jaundiced view of certain issues. Thus when somebody suggested to them that certain things should be done by very unorthodox policy they said "Oh, what the hell, let it go forward". ' Now I suppose we would all agree that, *if* that were true—it probably isn't— it would be a cause. And yet I do not think that economists would want to weave that into their theory of the causes and conditions of inflation.

Now I come back to our little controversy. We all, I think, agreed with you—there hasn't been a dissident voice—that in 9 cases out of 10 when a condition of inflation persists, there is an undue expansion of expenditure—expenditure gingered up by an increased credit base. Where we disagreed, where there was a good deal of talk earlier, was to what extent you could think of possible kinds of behaviour within the economic system which could, so to speak, be combined in the conception of causation with the failure of the government to do its duty to maintain the standard of value. And that, in spite of all that has been said, I do believe in the end is a bit of a semantic question. Although you—and David Laidler— adduced evidence to persuade us that a great deal of what is said against trade union action is based on misapprehension, that some trade union action at any rate is vainly trying to keep up with relativities and the price level—you admitted to me that you knew you could have a slow explosion. And in conversation with Peter Jay we agreed that, if people got it into their heads that they were always going to ask for 105 per cent of the GNP, that would cause an indefinite expansion towards infinity which could only be stopped by the substitution of new money.

So are we really so much in disagreement? If I said that if, in the process of putting on the brakes on the rate of increase of money supply, some miracle occurred and the leaders of the Trades Union Congress passed a self-denying ordinance not during that period to do anything to maintain their position as they considered it ought to be, I do not think you would disagree that probably there would be rather less unemployment than there would be if they were in a frightfully aggressive mood. So where do we part company?

FRIEDMAN—I myself try to avoid the use of the word 'cause' for the very reasons you cite; it is a tricky and unsatisfactory word. When I use it in this connection I always speak of the change in the money supply as a proximate cause, and say that the deeper causes must be found in what are the explanations for the rise in the money supply. And yet I am not persuaded that the difference between us in these arguments is purely semantic. I believe there is a very real difference. It is brought out by your final case. Somehow or other the problem I get into is to try to distinguish analytical issues from practical issues. The final statement sounds to me like the following: if we may provisionally assume that water runs uphill, then will you agree with me that we will get more water to the top of the hill than otherwise.

LORD ROBBINS—No, I am not asking that, I am asking whether, if the conditions that prevailed in your Argentinian case were to occur in other times and in other places, there would not be an easier passage than if the reverse conditions prevailed.

FRIEDMAN—I agree they would. But then we have to face up to the analytical and empirical issues: under what circumstances can they prevail and under what circumstances do they prevail? I believe that it is an illusion of the worst kind to suppose that they always prevail, as both Brittan and Laidler have said. Suppose that this so-called income and price freeze is an example of the kind of thing you are describing. I think it was possible in Argentina to work it, partly because the rate of inflation was so extremely high, and partly because a government was able to persuade people that they were really going to conduct this policy, and as an adjunct to that it may have had some psychological effect—incidentally, trade unions were weak in your sense, not in the political sense but in an economic sense. If you could recreate those situations here it might have some effect. But I think in the real, concrete world it would not. Therefore there is a real difference.

But there are a couple of other points I would like to make, one deriving from David Laidler and one from Sam Brittan. You have the interesting phenomenon that whereas David Laidler came to Chicago, Chicago came to Sam Brittan. I must say there are few things that annoy me more, just as they annoy David Laidler, than the continual repetition of black box arguments. What is the mechanism? I have decided that the right way to answer those questions is simply to invite people to read David Hume's essay on money, because we must not think that we are discovering very many new things. About a year or so ago I was asked by the Bell Laboratories in New Jersey to talk to their scientists—not economists, but scientists of various kinds—about what we knew about money as part of a programme of bringing scientific contributions to their notice. In the course of preparing the talk I re-read David Hume's essay. And I must say I was in one respect very much depressed by it. There was so little I knew that was not there. We have not learned very much in two centuries. If anybody asks what is the mechanism whereby an increase in the money supply brings about an increase in prices, what David Hume has to say answers that question about as well as anything else I know. I ask myself, what do we really know that he did not know, and there is only a very little. We know the numbers better; we can attach numerical magnitudes; and we are a bit more sophisticated about the dynamic process of decelerating and accelerating inflation than he was; but beyond that he had it all.

Second, I recently re-read William Stanley Jevons's essay on the serious fall in the value of gold. And lo and behold I was shocked and again depressed by finding something I thought I had discovered. Jevons said an increase in currency is followed within a space of two years by an increase in prices. That was the lag he found in 1860. That is the lag I found in the United States. It's a lag that's true in Britain today. So that despite the increase in the speed of communication and in financial sophistication and so on, apparently the British and American lag and the adjustment of prices to an increase in the supply of money has remained unchanged.

LORD ROBBINS—You're not prepared to bet large sums of money on the continuance of that exact lag?

FRIEDMAN—No, that is where we know a little more. We know that the length of that lag depends on the rates of price inflation. In a world where people have been accustomed to relatively slow changes in prices, the two-year lag will prevail. As people become accustomed to more rapid changes in the rate of inflation, the lag will shorten.

The third historical reference I want to give you is J. E. Cairnes on the influence of the Australian gold discoveries.[1] He did something there which has been notably absent. He asked: if you have an increase in gold, which prices will react first, which second, which later? What will be the influence on relative prices of a general inflation? The fascinating thing is that his argument then would not hold water today, but the results he arrived at then have been pretty good from then to now. So far as I know nobody in recent times has explored that issue, either empirically in a systematic way or theoretically. He divided commodities into vegetable, animal and manufactured products. His analysis stemmed from the fact that the increase in the quantity of money in the first instance came into the hands of consumers. Whereas today all of our analysis proceeds on the assumption that it first goes into the credit market. So that the initial first round effect is wholly different, and yet the results seem to have been the same.

Finally, on Sam Brittan's question about mitigating hardship. I agree completely that the same total budget can be spread in ways which will alleviate hardship more or less. The policies I was writing about (in *Newsweek*) in the United States were not regional, but so-called public unemployment policies. And I submit to him that the policies that will be most effective to mitigate hardship will be improvements in unemployment measures for *long*-term unemployed. Avoid like the plague trying to do very much to improve the conditions for *short*-term unemployment because that is where you have the biggest leakage and the biggest extent to which you will increase the

---

[1] *Essays in Political Economy*, Macmillan, 1873, especially Essay II, pp. 53-66.

natural rate of unemployment. But if you take the very long-term hardship case, then I think there is a good deal to be said for mitigating it. I am very sceptical about the regional unemployment measures for doing it because it seems to me that much of that will be wasted, in shifting people who are employed rather than in assisting the people who most need assistance.

SUMMING UP

BY THE CHAIRMAN

LORD ROBBINS—I am surprised at the degree of apparent unanimity exhibited at this conference. As I said at the beginning, when we discussed this matter two years ago[1] we all agreed in deploring the effects of inflation, there was no one who argued that inflation was a jolly good thing, and should be promoted. (There have been—I am very sorry to say—professional economists in recent years who have sometimes said nearly as much as that.) But we did disagree a good deal more then than we have disagreed today about causes. I think that in private Professor Friedman and I could go on wrangling just a little bit about the division of responsibility between woolly-minded governments and their apprehension of the consequences of situations which they found politically inconvenient. But, apart from that, the degree of disagreement here has been very small indeed.

We have not had a long talk about wage and price controls. They have been alluded to from time to time, but very little has been said about the more detailed aspects of those consequences. In my opening remarks I think I ventured to say that I was a disbeliever in wage and price controls except as emergency measures. They always seem to me to break down and—as one speaker from the body of the hall said—they are a positive encouragement to a sort of cumulative dishonesty. Not only on the prices side: you can see that at the present time now if you go round on behalf of the family trying to get a little sugar in the shops. But still more on the incomes side, where those in charge of certain firms with deserving cases can think

---

[1] At an IEA Seminar in August 1972, subsequently published as *Inflation: Economy and Society*, IEA Readings No. 8, 1972.

of 101 ways in which the law can be disobeyed in spirit although in the letter it is still observed: renaming of jobs, revision of job specifications, and so on. The thing starts in a small way and it gradually breeds a contempt for the law all round.

As regards the short term, I accept Professor Friedman's statement that usually incomes policies have been accompanied by the thing which is bound to make them nugatory, namely a renewed inflation. Now I would never venture to interpret what happened in the United States, because one cannot interpret the United States unless one goes there once every two months or so. Certainly in our case the introduction of incomes policy was paralleled by the extraordinary burst of deficit financing which was the unfortunate result of the good intentions of the then Prime Minister and his Chancellor of the Exchequer. But I honestly do not believe that Mr Heath and Mr Barber introduced the prices and incomes control with the *intention* of inflation. I think they had a certain amount of schizophrenia in their thought in this way: they thought it would be a good thing to have prices and incomes control to deal with inflation, and then they thought, well, growth has been unsatisfactory and all sorts of people have been reproaching us for not having enough growth, so why should not we go for a bit of growth?

In the interpretation of British policy, for which I am not an apologist, which I continually attack in various ways, I would commend to you a remark of the philosopher Nietsche (who as you know was not as nice a man as he ought to have been—some of his remarks were absolutely abhorrent, particularly about women). But there is one aphorism which I have found a guide to many complicated phenomena in life:

'Not sin but folly'.

I now declare the conference closed.

Inflation, Full Employment and the Threat to Democracy*

PETER JAY

Economics Editor, 'The Times'

When, in 1980 or so, democracy as we know it has been suspended and people have accepted that the depression is established for a decade or so, the question may be asked, 'Where did we go wrong?' From that perspective could the disintegration of our political and economic comforts have been avoided?

Was the golden age of 'stop-go', as we used to call those 25 years of unprecedented and enviable prosperity, inherently unstable? Or did we just throw it away? Is it true that we did not appreciate it while we had it, complaining the while of 'slow growth' and of living standards that only rose two or three per cent a year? Can we call back yesterday, promising to complain no more and to respect the minimum conditions of its stability?

One of the boring things about 'if only' questions, when asked long after it is too late to profit from them, is that there is no way of testing the rival answers. The debate is endless and to no purpose. So there is, perhaps, some advantage in raising the questions now, hypothetical though strictly they must remain, since 1974 looks like being the year which future historians of the 'if only' school may identify as the moment when the last chances of fending off political and economic disaster were forfeited.

Why should we be talking about disaster at all? Certainly not because of any doom conceived by over-imaginative and under-rigorous amateur ecologists. Nor because of any predictable disturbance to the fabric of the world political order from without our own frontiers. Nor even—directly—because of some malignant extension of the progressive violence of our domestic social and political conflicts.

---

*Reproduced by kind permission of the Editor and the author from *The Times*, 1 July, 1974.

The irreconcilable quadrilateral

The reasons are much more systematic than any such random threats to everyday life, as most of us still think of it. They stem from the ever more palpable irreconcilability in the long-term—by now the not-so-long-term—of four essential features of our present political economy. Those features are:

1. Government whose authority rests on renewable popular consent;
2. The commitment to full employment—not just as an ultimate objective, but as a necessary requirement year by year and quarter by quarter;
3. The dependence on stable prices, or at least on stable rates of inflation or some stable basis of economic exchange; and
4. The durability of collective bargaining as the primary means of determining pay in the labour market.

The dangers of this quadrilateral were fully appreciated and carefully spelt out in the wartime coalition Government's Employment Policy White Paper of May, 1944, which established the commitment to full employment that has bound every subsequent Government. It cannot be quoted too often.

'If we are to operate with success a policy for maintaining a high and stable level of employment, it will be essential that employers and workers should exercise moderation in wage matters . . . The principle of stability does mean . . . that increases in the general level of wage rates must be related to increased productivity due to increased efficiency and effort. . . . The stability of these two elements [wages and prices] is a condition vital to the success of employment policy; and that condition can be realised only by the joint efforts of the Government, employers and organised labour. . . .

'It would be a disaster if the intention of the Government to maintain total expenditure [and thereby full employment] were interpreted as exonerating the citizen from the duty of fending for himself and resulted in a weakening of personal enterprise. For, if an expansion of total expenditure were applied to cure unemployment of a type due, not to absence of jobs, but to failure of workers to move to places and occupations where they were needed, the policy of the Government would be frustrated and a dangerous rise in prices might follow.'

That, in a nutshell, is the history of Britain's post-war economy, the rhetoric being endlessly repeated while the warnings were ignored and the forebodings were fulfilled. This degeneration was masked for nearly 25 years, partly by the delusory power of short-term economic cycles and partly by the preoccupation with Britain's inadequate growth rate.

The short-term cycles enabled people to believe that with one leap the economy was about to be free of whichever aspect of its chronic dilemma most immediately troubled it without recognising that this escape would merely aggravate another aspect of the basic quadrilateral of irreconcilables. When unemployment seemed to rise, reflation was expected to restore full employment without rekindling inflation. When inflation surpassed tolerable limits, deflation—or, more beguilingly, disinflation—was expected to restore stable prices without prejudicing full employment.

When the sterility of this see-saw was perceived—as from time to time it was (by Sir Stafford Cripps in 1948, by Mr Harold Macmillan in 1956, by Mr Selwyn Lloyd in 1961, by Mr Harold Wilson in 1966, and by Mr Edward Heath in 1972)—a third dimension was introduced perpetuating the delusion that the dilemma could be escaped, the problem solved. This dimension—known as 'incomes policy'—rested on that original perception in the 1944 White Paper that 'if we are to operate with success a policy for maintaining a high and stable level of employment, it will be essential that employers and workers should exercise moderation in wage matters . . .'

The delusion lay not in the analysis, which was entirely correct, but in the belief that such restraint could ever become a permanently effective feature of an open political economy such as ours. The difficulty was implicit in the dual requirement, again spelt out in the 1944 White Paper, for flexibility of relative wages and for stability of average wages.

Mr Enoch Powell has often asked the question of incomes policy advocates: 'How do you control the average without controlling individual pay; and if you control individual pay, how do you decide what it should be and how do you provide for the necessary flexibility on relative pay?' No durable answer has ever been found, though many institutions have been spawned and much bombast has flowed in the effort to solve that conundrum.

What the post-war experience demonstrates is that you can control average pay for a while at the cost of rigidity and anomaly in relative pay. But those rigidities and anomalies are not tolerated for more than a year or two; and then when they are rectified, the control over average pay inevitably collapses.

So policy has cannoned round, like a billiard ball, trapped in the triangle of deflation, reflation and incomes policy, somehow managing to keep alive the hope that this time it is going to be different, that the economist's stone has been found and that all requirements will be satisfied simultaneously by the end of the 'forecast period', that ever-receding horizon of economic salvation.

That delusion has been compounded by the diversion of critical and sceptical attention to the problem of slow growth, reflecting the ingenuous belief that 'stop-go' was an evil, born of amateurism in the Treasury or cowardice in Downing Street, which needed to be displaced in favour of a better performance called 'sustained growth'. 'Stop-go' being an evil, or at least a failure, few bothered to ask whether it was itself a stable condition, whether we could indefinitely maintain it even if we wished to, whether indeed the future might not hold something much worse rather than something slightly better.

Yet, to anyone who could lift his gaze above the delusory vistas suggested by optimistic straight-line extrapolation of short-term economic spasms, who could see the secular trend through the cyclical motions and who could forget the fascination of faster growth, the pattern was clear. Things were getting worse, in the sense that the price of full employment was faster and faster inflation, while the half-life of incomes policies—and of the Governments which applied them—was getting shorter and shorter.

Progressive deterioration

The analysis on which this assertion rests was set out on this page on 5 December last year, from which the Table is taken, slightly updated. When this evidence of contracting scope for economic

POST-WAR CYCLES	I	II	III	IV	V
Period	**1952-57**	**1958-61**	**1962-65**	**1966-70**	**1971-73**
Duration	6 yrs	4 yrs	4 yrs	5 yrs	3 yrs
Real GNP rise (%)	16·4	12·1	13·4	11·2	10·9
Peak Unemployment (b)	1·8	2·0	2·2	2·3	3·7
(% average for year)	(1952)	(1959)	(1963)	(1968)	(1972)
Peak inflation (a)	5·3	3·4	4·7	6·4	9·2
(% year-on-year)	(1955)	(1961)	(1965)	(1970)	(1973)
Peak Payments (c)	0·91	1·12	1·29	‡	2·07
Deficit (% of GDP)	(1955)	(1960)	(1964)		(1973)

‡Masked by 1967 devaluation.
(a) Change in average retail price level between calendar years.
(b) Unemployed in GB excluding school-leavers and adult students.
(c) Current account in calendar years.

manoeuvre is taken with Sir Richard Clarke's research report ('Incomes Policy in Phase Four') for the Centre for Business Research last year, depicting the rise and unavoidable fall of the four previous post-war incomes policy cycles (to which we can now add the fall of the fifth), it is amazing how much of post-war economic discussion has been devoted to the search for an improvement upon past performance rather than to finding means of arresting its deterioration.

If then the three sides between which our policy billiard ball has been ricochetting are in fact converging—as everyone tries harder and harder to secure the purchasing power of his income at a level significantly above the value of what he is producing by pushing his pay up faster than his pay pushes up the prices he pays—what happens when the ball is finally wedged and can move no more?

Collapse of democracy

What happens is that the fourth indispensable feature of our political economy—namely democracy—collapses. For, by hypothesis, prices are by then rising faster than people will tolerate from a Government which they can remove. Unemployment is by then higher than people will tolerate from a Government which they can remove. Incomes policy is at the end of its latest cycle and cannot for the time being be revived by a Government which people can remove.

As Dr Otmar Emminger, the world renowned seer of West Germany's central bank put it in London on 17 June, 'unbridled inflation is a sane way to the ungovernability of a country—at the end of the road there loom controls, dirigism and loss of freedom —it is also a sure way for Governments towards political suicide'. But so also is resistance to inflation.

All roads are blocked. All delusion is at an end, since the billiard ball is no longer in motion; and so even the most devout optimists can no longer believe that it is heading for the open spaces of stable economic progress. Governments not only cannot square the circle of full employment with stable prices and collective bargaining; but also it is seen that they cannot.

So they are no longer tolerated, even for short probationary periods such as our present Government has been permitted. Everyone is in arms against the injustice, against the chaos and above all against everyone else's pet solutions.

It is futile to try to predict exactly when this moment will be reached, as it is to try to describe the exact chain of political events which will show the eventual breakdown of government depending on popular consent. My own guess is that we may stagger round one more economic cycle, perhaps two, and that something should be allowed also for the tendency of logic always to take rather longer to work itself out in Britain than one expects. But 1980, give or take a couple of years, seems to me a cautious-to-middle view.

How could it be avoided? Only, it appears, by first suspending at least one of our four irreconcilables. But by hypothesis that is not possible. Governments depending on consent cannot suspend the full employment commitment. They cannot accommodate society to inflation accelerating to hyper-inflation, even if that is what society prefers, because there must be some medium of exchange and that medium will be progressively debased so long as we can stipulate and get rewards in excess of what we produce.

Nor can such governments for long suspend or interfere with collective bargaining for reasons which are as obvious after the events of the past five years as they are hard to prove.

But, it will be objected, if it is the imperatives of popular consent which, combined with the facts of economic life, create the dilemma and lead to the disaster, why cannot they be changed, be changed indeed by telling people of their consequences? If only it were so easy. But people *have* been told, beginning in the 1944 White Paper and repeatedly in just about every pronouncement by every Chancellor and other economic authority ever since.

The warnings are not heard. If heard, they are not believed. If believed, they are not thought to apply to the special circumstances of the believer. There is no way that a generation nurtured in political scepticism, yet recognising no limits to the demands which it makes of the Governments which it holds in such contempt, can be persuaded by further doomladen words that danger approaches. They have heard it before; and it has not happened yet, as the man who fell from the top of the Empire State Building remarked on passing the tenth floor without mishap—yet.

Disinflationary policies the only solution

The only way that the disaster can be avoided is for the Government resolutely to pursue disinflationary (though not contractionary) policies and for the country to back them in doing so by accepting the means as well as by willing the ends. As Dr Emminger explained in London: 'If we want to get the inflationary excesses . . . out of our system, we will have to run the economy for a while at a little less than full steam.'

He was welcoming the evidence that this was happening in the United States and West Germany. But the moral is even more strongly applicable to Britain and the other high-inflation countries of Western Europe, where no such modification of the full employment commitment has been contemplated.

But it is essential to understand what that pleasant euphemism means. It means for Britain balancing the budget (subject to any acceptable 'oil deficit' on the balance of payments financed by foreign borrowing) and keeping the growth of the money supply in single figures.

Such policies interacting with the kind of first white- and then blue-collar pay explosion which looks inevitable this autumn would put extreme pressure on industry and produce a very sharp rise indeed in unemployment next winter and next year. If we are prepared to accept unemployment in the low millions for the rest of this decade, it is possible that inflation will be brought under control, that an incomes policy which offers employment rather than a vague hope of more stable prices in return for pay restraint will prove to have a much longer half-life than its ill-starred predecessors and that the forms of democracy can be preserved.

But, of course, that 'if' begs the whole question. At this particular moment the posture of budgetary and monetary policy is not particularly inflationary. But the choice will arise very soon when the autumn's pay explosion begins to price large numbers of people out of their jobs and the Government comes under intense pressure to reflate in order to check unemployment.

It is hardly imaginable that it will not respond to that call or that, if by some political freak it did not, it would not be rapidly removed from office in favour of some other administration promising quick action against unemployment. So we can take the next plunge into large budget deficit and all-out monetary expansion for granted.

Moreover, this next bout of super-inflationary underwriting of super-inflationary pay demands will start when prices are already rising at about 15 per cent a year, a figure which would probably be nearer 20 per cent if industry were free to pass on all the cost increases it has suffered. When that plunge is taken, probably in Mr

Healey's promised second budget followed by other reflationary measures through the winter, that last chance of stabilising our economic life under democratic governance will be gone. As Dr Emminger said, 'the outlook is very dark at present'.

Admittedly he went on to discern 'a ray of light at the end of the tunnel'. But that turned out to be the determination of the United States and of West Germany to fight inflation, partly because of West Germany's celebrated 'abnormal sensitivity against inflation' and partly because 'the United States trade unions have refrained at least up to now from putting a wage-cost inflation on top of the cost inflation from energy and raw material prices'. No such rays are visible in Britain or indeed in most of the other West European industrial countries.

Economic performance and political institutions

Although the basic mechanics of the inflation which destroys democracy are domestic and theoretically within national control, given the popular political will, the problem is by no means confined to Britain. The timing of political breakdown depends on the interaction of economic failure on political institutions. Countries with bad economic performance and strong political institutions may, therefore, not suffer political collapse before countries with better economic performance and weak political institutions.

Countries like Italy which are weak in both ways naturally succumb first. Countries like the United States and perhaps Switzerland which are strong in both ways may never succumb at all. Countries like Britain, France, Japan and West Germany, which are strong in one respect, but weak in the other, come between the first two groups.

When we come to look back a decade or so from now on that quarter century of democratic prosperity after the Second World War, it will no doubt seem amazing that its indefinite perpetuation was so widely taken for granted and that the dangers were so little recognised. Even more surprising will be how little it was appreciated while it lasted and how bitterly its achievements, both political and economic, were dismissed.

Inflation: the Path to Unemployment*

F. A. HAYEK

Nobel Laureate 1974

I

The responsibility for current world-wide inflation, I am sorry to say, rests wholly and squarely with the economists, or at least with that great majority of my fellow economists who have embraced the teachings of Lord Keynes.

What we are experiencing are simply the economic consequences of Lord Keynes. It was on the advice and even urging of his pupils that governments everywhere have financed increasing parts of their expenditure by creating money on a scale which every reputable economist before Keynes would have predicted would cause precisely the sort of inflation we have got. They did this in the erroneous belief that this was both a necessary and a lastingly effective method of securing full employment.

'Seductive doctrine'

The seductive doctrine that a government deficit, as long as unemployment existed, was not only innocuous but even meritorious was of course most welcome to politicians. The advocates of this policy have long maintained that an increase of total expenditure which still led to an increase of employment could not be regarded as inflation at all. And now, when the steadily accelerating rise of prices has rather discredited this view, the general excuse is still that a moderate inflation is a small price to pay for full employment: 'rather five per cent inflation than five per cent unemployment,' as it has recently been put by the German Chancellor.

This persuades most people who do not see the grave harm which inflation does. It might seem—and even some economists have maintained—that all inflation does is to bring about some redistribu-

---

*Reproduced by kind permission of the Editor and the author from the *Daily Telegraph*, 15 and 16 October, 1974.

tion of incomes, so that what some lose others will gain, while unemployment necessarily means a reduction of aggregate real income.

This, however, disregards the chief harm which inflation causes, namely that it gives the whole structure of the economy a distorted, lopsided character which sooner or later makes a more extensive unemployment inevitable than that which that policy was intended to prevent. It does so by drawing more and more workers into kinds of jobs which depend on continuing or even accelerating inflation. The result is a situation of rising instability in which an ever-increasing part of current employment is dependent on continuing and perhaps accelerating inflation and in which every attempt to slow down inflation will at once lead to so much unemployment that the authorities will rapidly abandon it and resume inflation.

We are already familiar with the concept of 'stagflation' to describe that state in which the accepted rate of inflation no longer suffices to produce satisfactory employment. Politicians in that position have now little choice but to speed up inflation.

Disorganisation of economic activity

But this process cannot go on for ever, as an accelerating inflation soon leads to a complete disorganisation of all economic activity. Nor can this end be avoided by any effort to control prices and wages while the increase of the quantity of money continues: the particular jobs inflation has created depend on a continued rise of prices and will disappear as soon as that stops. A 'repressed' inflation, beside causing a still worse disorganisation of economic activity than an open one, has not even the advantage of maintaining that employment which the preceding open inflation has created.

We have in fact been led into a frightful position. All politicians promise that they will stop inflation *and* preserve full employment. But they *cannot* do this. And the longer they succeed in keeping up employment by continuing inflation, the greater will be the unemployment when the inflation finally comes to an end. There is no magic trick by which we can extricate ourselves from this position which we have created.

This does not mean that we need go through another period of unemployment as we did in the 1930s. That was due to the failure to prevent an actual shrinkage of the total demand for which there was no justification. But we must face the fact that in the present situation merely to stop the inflation or even to slow down its rate will produce substantial unemployment. Certainly nobody wishes this, but we can no longer avoid it and all attempts to postpone it will only increase its ultimate size.

The only alternative we have, and which, unfortunately, is a not unlikely outcome, is a command economy in which everyone is assigned his job; and though such an economy might avoid outright worklessness, the position of the great majority of workers in it would certainly be much worse than it would be even during a period of unemployment.

Market economy not at fault

It is not the market economy (or 'the capitalist system') which is responsible for this calamity but our own mistaken monetary and financial policy. What we have done is to represent on a colossal scale what in the past produced the recurring cycles of booms and depressions; to allow a long inflationary boom to bring about a misdirection of labour and other resources into employments in which they can be maintained only so long as inflation exceeds expectations. But while in the past the mechanism of the international monetary system brought such an inflation to a stop after a few years, we have managed to design a new system which allowed it to run on for two decades.

As long as we try to maintain this situation we are only making things worse in the long run. We can prevent a greater reaction than is necessary only by giving up the illusion that the boom can be prolonged indefinitely and by facing now the task of mitigating the suffering and preventing the reaction from degenerating into a deflationary spiral. It will chiefly be a task not of preserving existing jobs but of facilitating the opening of (temporary and permanent) new jobs for those who will inevitably lose their present ones.

We can no longer hope to avoid this necessity, and closing our eyes to the problem will not make it go away. It may well be true that because people have been taught that government can always prevent unemployment, its failure to do so will cause grave social disturbances. But if this is so, we probably have it no longer in our power to prevent this.

II

In order to see clearly the causes of our troubles it is necessary to understand the chief fault of the theory which has been guiding monetary and financial policy during the past 25 years. It is the belief that all important unemployment is due to an insufficiency of aggregate demand and can be cured by an increase of that demand.

This is the more readily believed as it is true that some employment is due to that cause and that an increase in aggregate demand will in most circumstances lead to a temporary increase of employment. But not all unemployment is due to an insufficiency of total demand or would disappear if total demand were higher. And, worse, much of the employment which an increase of demand at first produces cannot be maintained by demand remaining at that higher level but only by a continued rise of demand.

This sort of unemployment which we temporarily 'cure' by inflation, but in the long run are making worse by it, is due to the misdirection of resources which inflation causes. It can be prevented only by a movement of workers from the jobs where there is an excess supply to those where there is a shortage. In other words, a continuous adjustment of the various kinds of labour to the changing demand requires a real labour market in which the wages of the different kinds of labour are determined by demand and supply.

Without a functioning labour market there can be no meaningful cost calculation and no efficient use of resources. Such a market can exist even with fairly strong trade unions so long as the unions bear the responsibility for any unemployment excessive wage demands will cause. But it disappears once government relieves the unions of this responsibility by committing itself to the maintenance of full employment at any price.

Role of the unions

This, incidentally, also answers the very confusing dispute about the role of the unions in causing inflation. There is, strictly speaking, no such thing as a cost-push inflation: all inflation is caused by excessive demand. To this extent the 'monetarists' led by Professor Milton Friedman are perfectly right. But unions can force a Government committed to a Keynesian full employment policy to inflate in order to prevent the unemployment which their actions could otherwise cause; indeed, if it is believed that the Government will prevent a rise of wages from leading to unemployment, there is no limit to the magnitude of wage demands—and indeed even little reason for the employers to resist them.

There is a little more reason to question Professor Friedman's recommendation of indexing as a means to combat the current inflation. No doubt indexing could do a lot to mitigate the harm inflation does to such groups as pensioners or those who have retired on their savings. And it might even cure at the root such inflations as are due to the inability of a government to keep up revenue to cover current expenditure.

But it is not likely to remedy the present inflation which is due to all people together trying to buy more than there is on the market and insisting that they be given enough money to enable them to buy at current prices what they expect to get. In this they must always be disappointed by a new rise of prices caused by their demand, and the vicious circle can be broken only by people contenting themselves with a somewhat lower real buying power than that which they have been vainly chasing for so long. This effect, however, a general adoption of indexing would prevent. It might even make a continuous inflation inevitable.

But at present it is not chiefly wage demands that drive us into accelerating inflation—though they are part of the mechanism that does so. But people will learn before long that the increase of money wages is self-defeating. What is likely to drive us further on the perilous road will be the panicky reactions of politicians every time a slowing down of inflation leads to a substantial rise of unemployment. They are likely to react to it by resuming inflation and will find that every time it needs a larger dose of inflation to restore employment until in the end this medicine will altogether fail to work. It is this process which we must avoid at any price. It can be tolerated only by those who wish to destroy the market order and to replace it by a Communist or some other totalitarian system.

'Face the facts'

The first requirement, if we are to avoid this fate, is that we face the facts, and make people at large understand that, after the mistakes we have made, it simply is no longer in our power to maintain uninterrupted full employment. No economist who has lived through the experience of the 'thirties will doubt that extensive and prolonged unemployment is one of the worst disasters which can befall a country. But all we can hope to do now is to prevent it from becoming too extensive and too prolonged and that it will be no more than an unavoidable period of transition to a state in which we can again hope to achieve the reasonable goal of a high and stable level of employment.

What the public must learn to understand if a rational policy is to be possible is that, whatever may be the fault of past Governments, in the present position it is simply no longer in the power of government to maintain full employment and a tolerable productive organisation of the economy.

It will need great courage—and almost more understanding than one dares to hope for—on the part of the Government to make people understand what the position is. We are probably approaching a critical test of democracy about the outcome of which one must feel apprehensive. One of the prime requirements of its successfully weathering this crisis is that the people are in time undeceived about the fateful illusion that there is a cheap and easy means of at the same time securing full employment and a continuous rapid rise of real wages. This can be achieved only by that steady restructuring of the use of all resources in adaptation to changing real conditions which the debauching of the monetary medium prevents and only a properly functioning market can bring about.